Secrets of Sizzlin' Sex

for Naughty but Nice Women Everywhere

The Take Charge,
Batteries not Included,
Beducation Handbook
of Steamy Sensuality
& 100% Safe Sex,
With or Without
a Red-Hot Lover.

As revealed by those Buzzin' Babes . . .

Cricket Richmond and Ginny Valletti

HOURGLASS
BOOK PUBLISHING

(dist by PGW)

Hourglass Book Publishing is a division of Marketscope and Hourglass Book Publishing, Inc. (P.O. Box 171, Aptos, CA 95001)

Notice:
As presented, the suggestions and/or positions in this book are safe and satisfying for the majority of adult women and men. Since every person is physically unique, some positions and/or products may not be suitable for your personal use. In this regard, please respect your body and honor its capabilities. If you have any questions about your physical or sexual limitations, consult a physician. Neither authors, publisher nor distributor can be held responsible for persons who may receive any injury from suggestions contained herein. While we have found certain products to be helpful and enjoyable, we are in no way endorsing a specific product nor are we assuming any product liability. The choices and responsibility belong to the reader.

Foreword

Once Upon a Fantasy

By: _____ (your name)

It was a sultry, starlit night. I sighed breathlessly as
_____ (your real/fantasy
lover's name) moved his hot, muscular body rhythmically above mine. Faster, harder, deeper he thrust
his manhood into me, filling the depths of my being.
Within seconds he moaned, groaned and climaxed
with a force that made the earth move. "Darling, was
it as good for you as it was for me?" he whispered.
Voice quivering, I replied . . . _____

_____

(Fill in *your* outcome.)

PSSST . . . Come a little closer . . . I've got some questions to ask you. **How's your sex life?** Have you been living hot, lusty fantasies or are you still reading romance novels and wishing some-day your prince will come . . . and so will you? Isn't it time you stopped dreaming about ectasy and started experiencing the or gasms you deserve?

Want to "wow" yourself and/or some lucky man with your pas-sionate panache? *Secrets of Sizzlin' Sex* will teach you the un-bridled erotic *expert-tease* necessary to help every woman turn her body into a finely tuned instrument for sexual gratification. Once you master the easy-to-learn intracacies of self-pleasure, it's a cinch to: 1) Get and keep the man you want, 2) delight the one you have, or 3) totally enjoy a love affair with yourself.

If your sex life's satisfying or just so-so, these seductive secrets will make it steamy. But if it's lacking, then this will light your fire. *Sizzlin' Sex* goes way beyond the hot stuff you may already know. In a playful, practical, easy-to-follow way, these handy tips will cata-pult you into a whole new world of orgasmic possibilities you never believed attainable!

Important . . . *Sizzlin' Sex* can be 100% safe sex! Learn to take mat-ters into your own hands and eliminate the fear of infection, rejection, unwanted pregnancy and hunks from hell.

Sizzlin' Sex awakens your sexuality and teaches you the skills necessary for pleasuring your significant self and/or significant other. This is *every woman's* handbook, no matter what age or stage of life. Whether you are . . .

- Single and wanting to mingle,
          but AIDS and other diseases
          scare the pants *on* not off you.
- Married but sex is infrequent, not *in*-frequent
           and b-o-r-i-n-g besides.
- Widowed a genital and gentle reminder:
           use it or lose it!

Share if you dare . . . or privately prepare to fulfill your every dream. Come with us now to the hotbed of playful erotica and outrageous orgasms . . . whether you have a partner or not. Learn everything your heart (and other good parts of your body) desires. In fact, we're so positive these *fun-damentals* will work sexual wonders, we offer this **Satisfaction Guarantee**.

FUN-OFFICIAL
CERTIFICATE

Satisfaction Guaranteed

If Not *Come-pletely* Satisfied
Your Orgasm Will Be Refunded!

_____   _____
Bare-er's Signature   *Sex-pert*

Attention, men! This book is ***not* for women only**. Inside *Sizzlin' Sex* you'll find everything you ever wanted to know about what turns women on . . . right at your fingertips.

"Women often have to give themselves permission to enjoy what they find pleasurable."
Beverly Whipple, Ph.D. (Foreword, *Ultimate Pleasure*)

"Sexual discovery about yourself by yourself is an unequated joy."
Barbara Debetz, M.D. & Samm Sinclair Baker (*Erotic Focus*)

"Whoever said orgasm wasn't important for a woman was undoubtedly a man."
Shere Hite (*The Hite Report*)

"It is only to be expected that women whose lovemaking entails faking, giving only for another, wind up viewing sex as a chore, a duty which is performed only in order to have children or keep a husband or lover from straying."
Lonnie Garfield Barbach, Ph.D. (*For Yourself*)

"If you can express what you really need and want without fear or shame, your desires are often met with surprising quickness."
Alexander Penny (*How to Make Love to Each Other*)

"Choosing to have orgasms any way you want is your right. Making them happen is your responsibility."
Eva Margolies

"I hate to brag, but if I were a man I'd love making love to me . . . come to think of it, I do love making love to me!"
G.S., Ft. Lauderdale, FL

"It won't take you long to realize that masturbation is a happy, healthy, normal act that can contribute to your well-being and sensuality enormously."
"J" (*The Sensuous Woman*)

"Remaining sexually active can actually slow some aging processes and protect the immune system."
Paul Pearsall, Ph.D. (*Super Marital Sex*)

"No woman can call herself free who does not own or control her body."
Margaret Sanger

"Too much of a good thing can be wonderful."
Mae West

Kisses & Kudos to the Following:

- ♥ All those candid, gutsy gals who have allowed us to share the secrets of their sex-capades.
- ♥ To naughty but nice women everywhere who deserve to have the best darn orgasms in the whole wide world . . . solo or shared.
- ♥ Sam, my lifelong friend/husband/lover, mentor to multiple orgasms and ever enthusiastic research assistant. *G.V.*
- ♥ To my passionate playmate "Stud Muffin." He encouraged us to write this book and lent me more than a helping hand. With him I laugh my way to orgasm and **sizzlin' sex** gets bedder and bedder. Thanks from the bottom of my heart . . . and other good parts. *C.R.*
- ♥ Thank you, thank you to "J." A very special woman whose blockbuster book, *The Sensuous Woman*, gave me and millions of women permission to get in touch with their own sexuality. Meeting you has been a high point in my life and an inspiration for writing this book. *C.R.*
- ♥ Our fabulous family, friends (especially Dedi) and literary lawyer, Sara Goodman.
- ♥ Oops, almost forgot my "was-been." Thanks for the divorce. It was the dawn of my sexuality and the rebirth of my life. *C.R.*

Who is "I" anyway?

You'll notice that when you begin reading this book there are stories of *sex-cess*, romantic antics, etc. that are in first person. How can that be in a book with two authors? Easy, "I" is either Cricket or Ginny. Sometimes you, the reader, will never really be sure. But soon the "I" will become a sensually satiated "you."

Contents

1

Secrets of Our Sex=cess

(With and Without a Man)

Fake Orgasm . . . You Bet I Did

What an act—a performance good enough to win an Oscar, Tony or darn near any other "guy." Just as convincing as that classic scene in the movie *When Harry Met Sally*. My starring role was played *tour de "farce"* during sex with my husband. The script was filled with pretend passion and generous amounts of moans, groans and gyrations. It was such a good show he never suspected (Did he even care?). The sad part was I didn't fool the most important person . . . **me**. As with a majority of women, I thought it was the man's responsibility to lead me to ecstasy.

Like Most Young Girls, I Dreamed Someday My Prince Would Come

He did, I didn't! At the ripe old age of twenty, I married him anyway believing all my problems, sexual and otherwise, would magically disappear. Wrong! Oh well, wasn't giving my partner pleasure all that mattered? Besides, didn't I have it all . . . you know, the great American dream: a house, children, designer clothes (at discount) and a successful career to boot? Continuing to play the part, I walked, talked and acted like a real hot number, fooling most of the people most of the time. Behind the scenes, sexual frustration was affecting my "storybook" life.

The Big "O" Was Often on My Mind

Where were those rapturous orgasms written about in romance novels? I'd have settled for a small one, but no luck. Meanwhile, my prince *not-so-charmingly* climaxed at the drop of my panties, while I, alas, remained a lady-in-waiting. Trying harder to jump-start my lagging love life, I pulled out all the stoppers: champagne, candlelight and every imaginable position short of hanging from a chandelier. I thought about putting mirrors over the bed but didn't want to see myself faking orgasms! When nothing worked, I shifted into high gear by exercising, dieting and bleaching my hair to see if blondes really have more fun. Ha! You can guess what happened—nadda, nothing, zippo. What to do, what to do?

Sure, I'd Heard About Masturbation

Back then, nice girls didn't mention *that* word, let alone *do it.* Especially if, as we used to believe, they had a man to give them orgasms. Concerned with keeping up appearances, I continued to act (since I wasn't able to react), but didn't dare discuss my ten years of frustration with family or friends. I honestly felt like the only woman on the planet who couldn't climax. Fed up and desperately seeking sexual satisfaction, this "nice girl" decided to try her hand at doing her own thing.

Literally and Clitorally, My Time Had Come

I remember clearly that eventful morning. After hurrying my husband off to work and carting the kids to school, I raced to the bedroom, plopped myself onto a plastic-covered recliner and masturbated for the first time. Instant ecstasy? Not exactly— my fingers cramped, a press-on nail got lost in the shuffle and I worked up a sweat, sticking to the darn plastic. Two hours into the mission, **Wow,** what an orgasm! Years of pent-up passion exploded and a dynamite, sensuous, satisfied woman emerged. Joyously, a new chapter in my life began.

No Longer Faking It, Happily Making It

Unfortunately, I didn't share my secret pleasure with the "prince." I know now that mutual masturbation could have salvaged our sex life, perhaps saved the marriage . . . naah, even counseling couldn't do that. To celebrate my divorce, I finally had mirrors installed over my bed to reflect the *real,* sexy me.

I Began a Long Overdue Love Affair with Myself

I realized that before getting into a healthy relationship with a man, I first had to have one with myself. During self-pleasuring, I created wondrous ways to make my sex life totally outrageous and fulfilling. Once confident with my self-taught skills, I looked forward to sharing them with a significant other. No man in the picture? No problem, my sex life wasn't placed on hold. When I felt a little ahh horny, there was no need to do the bar scene searching for "Mr. Right," or make a rash decision about having unprotected sex with a new beau (due to AIDS and other anti-social diseases). I learned then what I espouse today: rather than gamble on the state of a man's health, take time getting to know him. After all, being in charge of one's own sexuality is the safest bet of all!

LISTEN UP LADIES . . .

- ♥ Men love it when we're sexually savvy and uninhibited (trying to work us up, they usually peter out).

- ♥ Turn yourself on, then if you have a playmate show him and he'll adore you for it!

- ♥ Becoming sensuous has its own rewards; do it for the joy you'll receive whether you have a partner or not.

- ♥ Mutual masturbation is a sizzlin', safe way to share sex with a new lover, spice up a dull routine, or make super sex steamier.

Billions and Billions of Orgasms Later, I'm Still Doing My Own Thing

Over the years, I devised thousands, well, maybe hundreds of ways, to indulge in romantic antics. Like tennis (my *second* favorite sport), I've made sex a playful pastime. The more I practiced, practiced, practiced, the better it got. The result:I've had more than my share of delightful men worship at my flat feet and go bonkers over my *sexpert-ease*. Bewitched by these techniques, they never want to leave. I don't know about your looks, but if my thunder thighs, black roots and other less-than-perfect attributes don't turn Romeos away, then these ideas will work for everyone! Believe me, it has nothing at all to do with physical beauty. Practice these sizzlin' secrets and keep your mate home playing, not straying.

I Learned to Take Matters into My Own Hands and Knew Other Women Could Too

After getting my sexual act together, I sincerely wanted to help other women by sharing my knowledge. I opened a unique boutique, the first ever to *tastefully* display and sell adult accouterments along with upscale gifts. To make the toys tempting yet less embarrassing to buy, I repackaged them in playful, non-intimidating ways. Another reason for the shop's enormous popularity was I explained how the goodies and gadgets could be enjoyed, with or without a partner, in a personal, but non-threatening style. Relieved at having someone understanding to talk to, countless women (married and single) revealed the sad state of their sex lives.

BELIEVE IT OR NOT . . .

- The average length of penetration during intercourse is a "whopping" 21/2 minutes.

- Only 25% of all women climax by penis stimulation alone.

- 75% of women can't orgasm by intercourse alone.

- 99% of women who masturbate become orgasmic.

- The less sex, solo or shared, a woman has, the less responsive she comes; in other words, use it or lose it.

Sex Isn't All It's Cracked Up to Be

Irrespective of their marital status, the majority of women were—here we go again—*faking it*. They described spending night after disappointing night making exaggerated displays of pleasure when they would rather have been sleeping, shopping—anything else—except being in bed with their mates. I explained how easily, effectively and enjoyably they could have the sexual satisfaction they desired. Embracing these methods, overwhelming numbers experienced immediate results. Spurred on by the positive effects my suggestions were bringing to their sex lives, I became certified in group facilitating, started women's sexuality support groups and began *pubic* . . . oops, public speaking.

Eroticism
1 Ohhh 1

I wanted to broaden my horizons, but the store's success encompassed all my time. Accepting an offer I couldn't refuse, I sold the business, packed up lock, stock and vibe then moved south. My plan was to spend more time motivating women on taking charge of their sexuality in a playful and practical way. As luck would have it, I met my co-author and business partner. At that time, Ginny was presenting self-love workshops, tossing in tidbits on keeping sexual excite-ment in relationships. She walked her talk, sharing secrets of her successful twenty-five-year marriage. Besides using an array of playthings, often times their repertoire

INSTANT SEX-PERT

"Marilyn" was sixty-eight and resigned to living her life never experiencing orgasm. She'd been unhappily married for forty years (partly due to lack of sexual satisfaction) when she called for a consultation. In the quick-fix, one-hour session (which is all it takes), I explained the benefits of using sexual toys and ploys on herself. Then when confident, I suggested making a date with her estranged husband to share them with him.

After a month, she called back sounding ecstatic, vibrant and giggling like a kid—she was having cataclysmic climaxes. Soon afterwards, she got the courage to include her astounded mate in on some super, mutually satisfying sessions.

Later, she sent a postcard from the Poconos signed, "The Torrid Trio." Marilyn, hubby and *hum-dinger* of a toy were having a ball on their second honeymoon!

A scene from a play? Nope. It's real, live drama — the human sexual response in action . . . yours, mine, every body's. We're programmed to have orgasms—lots of them. Our bodies were created to receive and react to erotic arousal. Here's how a leading lady—**you**—choreographs the staging of this *sex-ccessful* show.

The Four Phases of Eve . . . Evelyn . . . Every Woman

Most all of us have the physical ability and desire for orgasm. Whether performing solo or partnered, our bodies undergo physiological changes in definite patterns or cues along the path to the big "O." This sequence is the build up and release of sexual tension. Kudos to Masters & Johnson who identified and described the four-star production as:

★ **Excitement**

★ **Plateau**

★ **Orgasm**

★ **Resolution**

Each phase leads to the next and varies in intensity and length with every sexual experience. They are generalized here, with a bit of playfulness thrown in for entertainment.

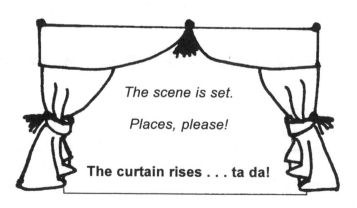

The scene is set.

Places, please!

The curtain rises . . . ta da!

Act I: Excitement

The opening number begins as your body takes its cue. Your system revs itself up, responding from sights, sounds, stimuli, etc. Another thirty seconds of prompting and the stars of the show prepare for their debut.

To top it all off, a flush may appear on parts of your body. Think I'm being overdramatic? Wait! This production is just getting underway as the physio-logical plot unfolds.

Act II: Plateau

If you or your leading man continues stimulation, excitement builds. Enter the plateau stage—a constant level of arousal. With continued prompting, your vagina gets wetter and wilder, fanning open to accommodate a finger, dildo or penis. The vagina's grand entrance becomes responsive to pressure and prodding, while the upper two-thirds remains fairly insensitive to touch. Breathing accelerates and your body throbs and swells to near bursting, yearning for release. **Wow!**

> **CAST OF CHARACTERS**
>
> **Vagina.**—reacts by lubricating and expanding.
>
> **Breasts**—get double billing; they swell, become supersensitive and the nipples perk up.
>
> **Heart**—the beat goes on and quickens.
>
> **Breathing**—gets heavier and faster (pant, pant).
>
> **Muscles**—tense from head to toe.
>
> **Nerves**—tingle and clamor for attention (more, more)!
>
> **Genital Lips**—dramatically unfold, exposing the vaginal entrance.
>
> **Clitoris**—this budding starlet becomes impassioned and excited.
>
> **Genital Area**—swells . . . and the spine-tingling presentation mounts.

Even though to this point your clitoris has been increasing in size, it now does a disappearing act, temporarily retracting from the limelight, hiding shyly under the hood, making it difficult to find. Not to worry! Stimulating your swollen labia lips and surrounding area moves the clitoral hood back and forth causing a flurry of excitement. While this is occurring, most experienced performers avoid touching the supersensitive head of their clitoris directly, opting to stimulate one side or the other to intensify the dramatic response.

Act III: Orgasm

Places, everybody! Get ready for the scene stealer. If stimulation continues, orgasm is likely to occur; if interrupted, excitement ebbs and may fade into the wings. This is especially true just prior to and during orgasm when continued stimulation is needed most. Rising to a fever pitch are your breathing, blood pressure and pulse rate. No matter how the grand finale is achieved—via man,

machine or self-manipulation—it is felt as a series of supercharged spasms. Your entire body is involved as you're catapulted to new heights. When contractions begin, each lasts less than one second, occurring about eight-tenths of a second apart, tapering off to slightly longer intervals. The scene's set for the final act . . . a mellow drama.

Act IV: Resolution

No, not the kind you make on New Year's Eve, because after each play, you may resolve to perform again and again, making this a long-running production. Then, unless you stage an encore, it takes thirty minutes or so for your system to calm and normalize. Your body goes limp and for a few minutes, at least, all is right in the real world.

Rave Reviews

Isn't it great being the woman starring in this live production? Bring down the curtain on a stellar, Stella . . . Ella . . . or _____ (*whatever your name is*) performance. You were maahh-valous!

Bravo, Darling!

Breasts—
A Tit-illating
Twosome

Thanks for the Mammaries

Call them what you will—boobs, hooters, jugs or knockers—the fact is breasts are a titillating twosome. Historically and hysterically, men have always had a preoccupation with mammary glands. We know, however, they're not just *man's breast friend* but, more importantly, contain lusty, busty possibilities for women.

Though not connected to any sex organ other than our brain, this dynamic duo is capable of responding rapidly to solo or partnered pampering. Still, most women bypass them in the rush to get down to business. Instead of hurrying your auto-erotic experience, s-l-o-w down and allow breast stimulation to be an upper persuasion for a lower invasion.

More Than Just a Booby Prize

Whether Dolly-dimensioned or luscious little love bumps, all breasts are fully loaded with sensory nerves that can be instantly activated. Size in no way symbolizes sexiness, touch sensitivity or reaction satisfaction. Although some females climax solely from breast arousal, most of us need additional nudging below the belt. Perhaps more women would take heart and hug those honey's if given some entertaining encouragement. Here then are some playful suggestions I'll get off my chest and onto yours.

Basic Breast Strokes: Here Are the Rubs

Note: Before taking matters into your own hands, create an enticing environment to enhance *response-ability* (see Chapter 9).

Start by erotically stroking under your arm with a fingernail or tip. Move slowly along the sides, sliding fingers down until slightly below the navel. Now make tiny circles around and under each breast as you teasingly come up. Repeat this light-handed approach several times.

The next step is a real pleaser. Cup and gently caress your entire breast and rotate in a circular motion, first one direction then the other. Linger lovingly, making this an unhurried, sensuous experience. Allow anticipation to build by continuously teasing yourself before targeting the exquisitely sensitive nipple.

Using whisper-soft touches, slowly spiral the dimpled areola. Keeping eyes closed, breathe deeply and focus in on the delicious feelings your tender loving caresses evoke.

Nipples are now becoming erect and can be coaxed further by strumming rhythmically. Using thumb and middle finger, fondle and playfully tug, twist, squeeze or roll those passion points. Experiment with different pressures. Firm handling, even to the point of pain, is preferable for some while others find light caresses more desirable.

Pallet-able Pleasures

Pretend your chest is a curvaceous canvas. Now dip an art brush into body paint or oil and sketch hearts, circles or outrageous designs. Fantasize your dream lover and allow creativity and inhibitions to run wild. Express your feelings with a flair and a flourish. Use a finger to write his name along with a sizzling message, tossing in naughty words for good measure. Don't forget to dot the "i's" and cross the "t's." Consider taking a close-up picture of your masterpiece and send it to your favorite art collector. This is one time you won't mind winning the booby prize!

A Material Girl

Get bare and dare to experience the feel of fabrics as you playfully fondle your pleasure chest. Give a little tickle using fur, feathers, satin or velvet. Hug a pillow covered in leather, lace or corduroy and brush vigorously back and forth against it. Wear leather, silk or an old flannel shirt and massage breasts through material.

Do your own thing while wearing a sexy bra. Especially erotic are those with *peek-a-boob* centers. These allow nipples to burst free while the lacy openings teasingly taunt perky peaks. Silk scarves, strands of pearls and other accessories are also titillating when swirled around naked skin.

Love Glove

I especially enjoy massaging my breasts while wearing latex gloves. The material imparts a silky feel that's indescribable. Imagining it's my lover's hand caressing me, optimizes the pleasure. For variety, don gloves made of lace, fur or leather.

Hot Ideas

Rubbing nipples with Ben-Gay® or similar heat-producing creams will warm more than your heart. Don't, however, use analgesic products on genitals. Better yet, purchase user-friendly **Hot Stuff** body oils and lavish them abundantly on bosoms. Feel your temperature rising as you lift mams to your mouth and gently blow. No oil available? Simply moisten a finger with saliva or sexy secretion and apply . . . hummmm.

Nip It in the Bud

Get humming by moving a battery-powered dildo around and between breasts. For an interesting effect, slip a "French Tickler Sleeve" (see *Dildos*, chapter 21) over the massager and let the textured nubs nip gingerly at your buds. For unrivaled stimulation, use an electric vibrator. (You have one, don't you?) If the vibe has multi-attachments, experiment and delight in the dizzying sensations each accessory imparts.

Terms of Endowment

"If your boobs hang low and wobble to and fro," make the most of your generous endowment. Lift a bountiful bosom to your lips and delight in giving yourself tender nibbles and kisses. Pour a few drops of chilled wine directly on those tasty tips, then bend down and blow dry. The combination of cold liquid and warm breath might get you high in a healthy, heady way.

Taster's Choice

For tempting treats, spread on whipped cream, honey, edible oils or other scrumptious goodies. Lick, flick and enjoy!

The Breast of Times

Having fun yet? By now, you've picked up a tip or two and are ready to bust loose. Go ahead, let your cup runneth over with pleasure!

Vagina— Non-Taxing Info

You have just received the letter on the next page from the I.R.S. Read it, and then proceed to read the rest of this chapter.

No Investment, No Return

Nobody likes being audited. We all know there are two things in life you can count on—death and taxes. Practically everything is levied, and although we pay, pay, pay, something new always gets added to the list. In states where the business of selling sexual gratification is legal, that too is taxed. So far there isn't an assessment for faking orgasm, but who knows, it may be next. At this writing, however, the only person getting cheated is the one who's faking it.

In preparation for a possible future tax on your very personal withholdings, the *Internal Revving-you Service* has devised an examination that points out invaluable vaginal hot spots. Form 1141 contains a winning combination of hands-on information to unlock orgasmic response. Obviously, if you don't know where the precious commodities are hidden, you can't reap the benefits. The I.R.S. is prepared to show you how to locate, activate and stimulate this treasure trove in a playful and rewarding manner.

Natural Endowments

An orgasm is an orgasm . . . right? Well, maybe, but how will you know until you've accounted for all your hot spots? Compare it to being awarded first place in a major sweepstakes. You've won the choice of: an all-expenses-paid trip around the world, $50,000 cash, or a new Mercedes complete with charming chauffeur to

Internal Revving-you Service
Intercourse, PA

RE: Notice of corrections and tax penalty

Dear Tax Player:
This agency has received reports of **withholding and/or faked vaginal orgasms** on previously filed 1140 forms. Check your past responses and verify authenticity. If we've made an error, please correspond and include a copy of the attached form VAG 1141. Without enhancements, your sexuality may be penalized. All tax players are entitled to an in-depth review of vaginal assets. The I.R.S. stands ready to offer helpful suggestions and assist in making beneficial recommendations. An audit can be arranged at your convenience to determine orgasmic *response-ability*.

Our principal concern is that you profit from this confidential exam. You have 14 days to get your self-sexual act together. Enclosed is our play-as-you-go form pointing out *fundamentals* for assessing your priceless vaginal vault and making rewarding improvements.

Sincerely,
R. U. Cheating

P.S.: Sexual freedom is protected under these guidelines. Failure to comply indicates of inhibitions and may cause a loss of orgasmic success. Remember, you owe it to yourself. You're worth it!

drive you wild. Which one's most advantageous for you? Tough choice. Likewise, orgasms, both clitoral and vaginal, are equally wonderful. Take your pick; you don't have to be limited. Luckily, the choice is yours, with variety being the winning ticket to enhancing sexuality.

Studies indicate that a majority of women fail to climax without sufficient clitoral stimulation which is A-OK. What's not appropriate is believing you can't orgasm vaginally without ever giving yourself the opportunity to learn. The *Internal Revving-you Service* offers valuable knowledge and assistance you'll profit from. This free, for-fun agency claims paybacks from vaginal climaxes are as satisfying as clitoral ones. If gratification from penetration is desired, then bottoms up to the I.R.S. because they offer solutions.

Examine Your Holdings

For starters, let's evaluate your anatomical assets. Visualize the shape of your eyebrows, nose and lips. Can you explain how they look? What color are your eyes? Easy questions, right? Now describe the shape of your labia lips. What color are they? You do know, don't you . . . I mean whose lips are they anyway? No doubt about it, our public face gets examined, pampered and observed all the time. We'd never think about taking those looks for granted. Our *pubic* structures are another matter. Most women are at a loss describing this prime property. Even if you're an expert at knowing what's up down there, check out this exam for its rewarding potentials.

C.P.A. = Certified Pubic Accountant

Being your own C.P.A. and taking account of the vaginal area is extremely beneficial. Besides the self-pleasure, enjoyment and increased response ability, you'll reap bonus credits for being open-minded. Enjoy yourself and, above all, don't cheat. This inquisition isn't meant to be taxing so playfully proceed as follows:

Form—check out the anatomy of your orifice.

Exam—explore the priceless assets stored within your vaginal vault.

Certification—note size and shape. Is it wet or dry?

Bottom Line—discover the combination to long overdue orgasms and unlock your sexuality.

An Audit You Outta Do

In a private, relaxed environment, sit with a mirror and flashlight or small lamp. Shine the light into the mirror and make the necessary adjustments so that you can view your vagina clearly. Squimish about hands-on self-exploration? Pop on a pair of surgical gloves and, if necessary, dab on a water-based lubricant. The diagram below will guide you, as one picture is worth a thousand words.

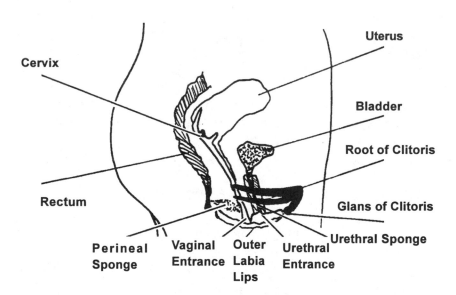

Without further delay, or at least before the April 15th deadline, review and answer the questions on the following form.

Form: VAG 1141   *Fun-official Inquiry*

PUBIC DOCUMENT

Name: _____   **Joint Return: Yes___ No___**

Instructions: Check off items inspected, making mental notes as you move along. Score and win $1,000 for playfulness. Subtract $1,000 for feeling guilty, embarrassed or turned off. Bailing out will cost you dearly.

1. Gently smooth back downy hairs around vaginal area. Pause and twiddle with its texture. ____

2. Are **outer labia lips** ruffled like an orchid and enfolded or pertly parted? What color are they? Will they stay open or are your lips sealed? ____

3. Notice shape and hue of **inner labia lips**—are they wet/dry, open/closed? ____

4. Slip a finger into the vagina, press inward then up towards the clitoris and search for a small bump. This is the **clitoral root** lying beneath the glans (the area outside that's visible). Press repeatedly watching the glans perk up in response. ____

5. Slide finger in further. Push down and forward feeling the **urethral sponge.** This thick layer of tissue surrounds the urethra and swells during arousal. Massage a while. Bingo, you've hit the G-spot! Got an urge to urinate? This too shall pass. ____

6. Tightly squeeze **vaginal muscle** to hug your finger. Now bear down and push out. If you can't feel pressure, start kegeling (Chapter 5) or tighten up with vaginal barbells. ____

7. Roll finger down and discover another spongy pad between vagina and anus called the **perineal sponge**. Massage the area for an unusual, yet sensual feeling ____

8. The vagina may be wetter than when first entered because its wall has started lubricating and loosening up. (You, too, hopefully.) ____

9. The vagina varies in depth from 2 to 5 inches and can stretch even more to fit a penis or dildo. Kneel down and reach in deep to locate the **cervix**. It sits at the top of your vaginal canal and feels like a small pearl dimpled in the center. During ovulation this dimpled area opens slightly. ____

10. Keep finger inserted then circle up, down and around massaging **vaginal wall**. Hopefully you'll hit the jackpot. ____

11. Remove fingers and breathe in love liquid covering them. Reap an additional $20 for being adventurous and adoring your million-dollar body. ____

Total: $10,000+ = Super Sensuous; $7,000+ = Very Sexy;
$5,000+ = Don't Worry, You'll Get It! $ _____

Give yourself a hug plus $2,500 bonus bucks for checking all blanks. Better yet, grab a vibrating dildo and go back for round two and more worthwhile *sex-plorations* in different positions.

Assessing Your Liquid Assets

In the peak of good health? If so, the vaginal lining will be moist, providing a healthy, protective coating. Even in an unaroused state, some degree of wetness is usually present. The quantity, however, is never consistent and varies depending on a woman's:

♦ Monthly cycle

♦ Age

♦ Level of stress

♦ Menopause

♦ General and genital health

♦ Degree of arousal

♦ Frequency of sexual involvement

Go With the Flow

Regularly being stimulated, excited, adored or amorously involved is the best way to keep you wonderfully wet. Seconds after arousal the vaginal wall produces numerous droplets of moisture. As sexual tension intensifies, liquidity increases forming a continuous lining of lubrication.

Dip Into Your Holdings

During manipulation, wetness may at times be lacking even though you're highly excited. This could be a result of lying on your back. In a prone position, gravity forces moisture to pool rather than flow down the vagina. Dipping a finger inside and moving it about helps bring love liquid to your opening. If there's still a short-fall, sit up or change positions until finding one that works.

Before making a deposit with finger, penis or love object, bank on one of the following lubricants to make vaginal penetration more rewarding.

DATE: TODAY'S THE DAY	**FUN FEDERAL BANK ♥** 101 PLEASURE LANE ANYPLACE, OH	ACCOUNT TYPE: *INTEREST* *BEARING*	DEPOSIT BOX *E-Z ACCESS* *E-Z INSERT*
TELLER APPROVAL: **YES** **YES** **YES**	NAME OF ACCOUTERMENT HOLDER _____ (Insert Your Name Here)	**TOY** DEPOSITS MADE WITHOUT LIQUID ASSETS MAY BE SUBJECT TO IRRITATION. IF ADDITIONAL LUBRICATION IS NECESSARY CHOOSE FROM : #1 INDIVIDUAL/SOLO #2 JOINT/SHARED	
☐ Individual ☐ Joint	***SLIP-IN DEPOSIT***	CHECK-OFF PRODUCT AVAILABILITY	
OPEN **24-HOURS**	*INSURED UP TO $1,000,000. ORGASMS* *MEMBER OF THE LAY BACK & DO IT CORP.*	***#1 INDIVIDUAL***	**(WATER SOLUBLE)** ASTRO GLIDE
	NOT RESPONSIBLE FOR:		K.Y. JELLY
	• SHORTAGE OF SATISFACTION	***#2 JOINT***	(NONOXYNOL 9)
	• LACK OF ORGASM		FOREPLAY
	• PENALTY FOR EARLY WITHDRAWAL		WET
		AVOID	**(do not insert)**
	*"BANK WITH **FUN***		EMOTION LOTIONS
	EXPERIENCE A PERPETUAL ♥ IN		MINERAL OIL
			PETROLEUM JELLY

Very Personal Trainer

Want to get yourself in shape inside and have fun doing it? I'm not talking Jazzercise® or aerobicise, but, would you believe, *vagacise*! Yes, you can add muscle to penetration using a mini metal barbell. This work-in wonder was devised to strengthen, tighten and tone the PC or vaginal muscle. Its weight, size and design make it a perfect *sexercise* item for women wanting to pump up self and shared pleasure. Get a wonder workout going in the comfort of your home without a handy gym or Jim dandy. Here's how to exercise your options:

1. Insert rounded end of barbell just inside vaginal opening. Initially it feels cold, making your vaginal muscle automatically contract. Within seconds, body temperature heats things up.

2. Use vaginal muscle to hug sphere tightly. As its weight creates resistance, this may take some training to achieve, but the payoffs are priceless. Release, then repeat for three sets of eight counts.

3. Squeeze barbell in even further then flutter muscle rapidly around it. Do three sets of eight reps.

4. Tightly grip barbell by flexing vaginal muscle. Focus and use control to draw it in, then push down and out *without using your hands*, giving this mega important muscle the conditioning it needs. Relax, you'll get it. Repeat two sets of six counts.

5. Lastly, use a hand to hold barbell and rotate in, out and about. Pretend you're working out with a live personal trainer. Add hip movements and visualize Arnie Schwartz, Arnold Swartzenegger or some other powerhouse of excitement coming your way, then get it on together.

F. Y. I.

In the *Hite Report*, a study of 3,000 woman, Shere Hite discovered, ". . . only 30% of women could orgasm regularly from intercourse . . . without more direct manual clitoral stimulation." And you thought you were the only one! However, women should know that the clitoral system is about 30% larger internally than externally, making the vaginal pathway a virtual hotbed of excitement. That's why so many hidden possibilities exist for women to become vaginally orgasmic. Fine tuning inner regions to be responsive takes desire, concentration and self-training. The key is to relax; rushing creates anxieties. Visualize, fantasize, let yourself go and lusty feelings will flow.

Feat Accompli

Think sexy and engage the biggest passion provoking organ of them all . . . your brain. Do whatever it takes to block out distractions and focus on fulfillment. Experiment and learn to be your own best lover. Sexually, most anything enjoyable with another can be reveled in alone. Being with yourself has advantages. For example, you don't have to think about blemishes, bulges, hair from hell, etc., making concentration easier. With or without a partner, forget perceived imperfections and explode ecstatically. Most men make love with greater abandon and success, because when they desire sex, they think orgasm . . . not lumps or love handles. Go ahead, give yourself permission to release pent-up sensuality, so it's randy, dandy and ready to share with the man of your dreams . . . lucky guy!

Play to the Order of

To up your chances of being vaginally orgasmic, consider using adult toys for penetration. Some of their advantages are:

- Your fingers may not be long or strong enough.
- Share them with a real playmate and enjoy 100% **safe sex**.
- Toys are always ready, willing and able.
- No partner? Dildos give a desirable feeling of fullness.
- Got a mate? Make it a threesome—you, him and your joy toy.

Get to vaginal payoffs pronto by diversifying your portfolio with one or some valuable commodities:

Don't "Pass the Buck" on this one!

#1
Battery-Operated Vibes*
Latex, Plastic, Silicone
Smooth/Textured
Curved/Straight
Hard/Soft
Rigid/Flexible

#2
Duo Combo
Man with Beaver
Pearl Diver
Finger & Thumb

#3
Electric and Rechargeable
Piston Action—up/down, in/out
Vibrators—multi-attachment
Wands with insertable tips

#4
Novel-Tease
Flex-a-Pleaser
G-Spotter
Sleeves & Add-ons
Vaginal Barbells

*Wide variety of shapes and styles that can be fitted with attachments. Drawbacks are that they're not always dependable, reliable or powerful enough for vaginal orgasms.

Tips You Can Bank On

Hesitant to use a dildo? If you want to be successful at having elusive vaginal orgasms, change your attitude. Get in on some safe, sexy, fun for one. Though it can't hug and kiss you, a dildo fills the bill while you learn orgasmic strategies. Here are some *in-valuable* tips:

- ♥ Name your dildo after a favorite tycoon, stock broker, celebrity or tax accountant. Pretend it's "him" inside helping you get deserved vaginal orgasms.
- ♥ Using music and erotica, make believe your joy toy's a live lover.
- ♥ Do *it* in the dark, wear a blindfold or use soft lighting.
- ♥ Learn from watching X-rated movies. Many adult videos portray women using dildos in a variety of positions.

Winning Positions

Numerous sex surveys show that most women experience penetration differently. What works well for one may not for another. Finding which performs best for you is of paramount importance. This is the reason why many books have been written on the subject. Invest worthwhile time and play around with a variety of key positions, such as:

Female Exec. (Women in Charge)

Shared: Lying face to face atop your partner leaves his hands free to explore your body and enables you to control movements and depth of penetration.

Pearl Diver

Solo: You're able to enjoy these same sensations using a finger or vibrating dildo such as the **Pearl Diver**. This position is rated A+ as it relaxes vaginal love areas, making them easier to reach and excite.

Game Time: A tennis partner of mine told me her favorite singles love match (off the courts) is using a bed pillow with arm rests. She selects a dildo then hops aboard the cushion, claiming its arms feel like a man's legs against hers. The firmness of the pillow combined with rhythmic thrusting is her winning combo to orgasm.

Kneel 'n Play

For an awesome reflection of your sensuality, kneel on a pillow in front of a full-length mirror. Watch admiringly as you pleasure yourself. Besides comfort, the pillow is perfect for holding a vibrating dildo such as the **Piston** with its up/down, in/out action. Flared based or combo dildos are preferable when kneeling. Position over one and thrust to your heart's content without worrying it will slip away. Keep your back upright and knees apart if you enjoy deep penetration; however, most sensitivity is within one to two inches of the entrance. Be a self-seducing voyeur and turn on to the sensuous woman in the mirror. See your image through the eyes of a lover.

Piston

Feet Accompli

Lying on your back, plant feet firmly against headboard or wall. This tenses pelvic muscles and tightens vagina adding pleasurable sensations. Strapping on the **Butterfly** or similar massager keeps tingly stimulation on the clitoris while freeing both hands to diddle with a dildo, finger or other fun thing.

Venus Butterfly

I told Henry, not tonight dear... I want to have an orgasm!

Different Strokes for Different Folks

Tall, short, big or small—one thing's for certain, every woman has a favorite position. To shed more insight on the subject, here are some quotes from everyday women like you and me:

Janet ❤ Single

"In order to climax vaginally, my legs need to be up and back, with my knees almost to my shoulders. Without a partner, I'll push my feet against the headboard, massage my boobs and use long, slow, penetrating strokes with a dildo."

Katie ❤ Married

"I've got to have smooth, rhythmic pumping. Position doesn't matter. In fact, I switch around quite a bit. Whether with my partner or some toy, I need to keep up steady vaginal stroking. Truthfully, I climax about 50% of the time, but since it feels good, I'm always satisfied."

Louise ❤ Divorced

"Watching X-rated flicks is my thing. With a favorite dildo pulsating inside, I'll be on my knees bent over a pillow and the video playing in clear view. Then I'll talk down and dirty to myself saying things such as 'You're really a (*Bleep*)' and, 'Get on that throbbing, hard (*Bleep*).' With a hoot 'n holler I climax."

Nicole ❤ Single

"Since finding my G-spot, I've become multi-orgasmic. However, I can only reach it on my knees, bending forward over a penis or a soft, curved dildo. Pressing my lower abdomen against my hand helps. I once dated a guy who had this upturned penis . . . it was fantastic feeling!"

Bev ❤ Married

"I need to be on top of my husband, aiming his erection to target my perfect spot. Initially, I'll do the thrusting, but as I start to climax, the passionate feelings overwhelm me and I stop. That's when he swings into action and starts pumping away, often resulting in multiple orgasms for me."

Doris ❤ Widowed

"Lying on my side I'll masturbate and have clitoral climaxes. They feel great, but I'm never fully satisfied without a dildo or penis inside to appease that empty feeling."

More on this from Shannon:

A SLICK CHICK AND HER CITY SLICKER

"How do I get vaginal orgasms . . . ahhh, let me count the ways! I used to believe that without a man, my sex life couldn't be satisfying. Although I never climaxed during intercourse, I enjoyed the feeling of a lover inside. One evening I was with a guy whose company and lovemaking really bored me when the following realization occurred: I'd rather be home watching *Gone with the Wind* for the twenty-second time, than waste another evening with unsatisfying intimacy. Fed up and disappointed by a string of unfulfilling relationships and concerned about safe sex, I started a quest toward personal pleasure.

My first move was replacing my hard plastic dildo with a realistic, flared base, vibrating one that I playfully named "Slick." Trying different positions, I kneeled face down with a pillow folded beneath me. The vaginal pressure felt fabulous. Swiveling my hips atop Slick, I'd heat things up further by massaging my clitoris. Raising up occasionally, I'd watch my breasts seductively swing with the rhythm. Then finding my *G-oodspot*, I'd prop Slick securely into the pillow, sink down onto "him" and let waves of pleasure engulf me. Sometimes I'll strap on a clitoral vibrator and get into all sorts of positions, while Slick or another rubber Romeo fills me up inside. I find inflexible and non-vibrating dildos as flat out boring as some of my previous dates. Until the right dude comes along, my macho collection consists of a variety of make-believe movers and shakers.

It's evident that with my confidence and libido in tact, men are more attracted to me. As a result, I'm not desperate for dates. Besides, being afraid of STDs makes me *very selective* about who to be intimate with. When my next relationship materializes, I'm certain it's going to be extremely gratifying.

Love,
Shannon

Scent-itive Subject

Mademoiselle, I love your smell!

Before ending this chapter on the vagina, I'd like to clear the air about a sensitive subject. We've been doing a number on dollars and cents, now let's move on to *dolls* and *scents.* Is there a woman out there who at one time hasn't worried about a lover being turned off by her womanly scent? Just as I thought, not a hand went up! Although most men admit they're turned on to the aroma and piquancy of a woman, the majority of females aren't comfortable about their intimate fragrance. Though a woman will perform oral sex on a man, she may not feel at ease allowing him to return the favor. Further nonsense—a woman may taste his ejaculate yet turn the other cheek at the thought of sampling her own essence. Assuming you know how you look "down there," it's time to go a dainty step further and discuss feelings regarding personal perfume. Hang in, relax, breathe normally . . . what I'm about to say hopefully won't take your breath away.

Common Sense

A rose is a rose and vaginal essence is an important part of our flowering sexuality. In many cultures, women as well as men consider personal aroma an alluring aphrodisiac. When our sexual hormones are pumping they produce a sort of musky smell similar to that used in some perfumes. Musk's popularity is due to its known potent affect of attracting members of the opposite sex.

Don't underestimate the nose as an erogenous zone. Contrary to what you may think, scents that entice many males aren't those of deodorants, but rather a clean, feminine fragrance. True, odors generated during sexual ardor are unique; that's why being comfortable with them depends as much on attitude as with the aromas themselves. Any healthy woman with adequate hygiene habits should be confident her fragrance is A-OK. That doesn't mean driving yourself crazy by douching. This only upsets the delicate vaginal pH balance essential to good health. Follow your nose, so to speak, when cleaning up your act. In essence, down 'n dirty is great for dancing, but keep *it* clean when romancing.

Now can you breathe easier? Until you become aware of and accept your personal aroma, you'll never be totally comfortable with physical intimacy. Change your attitude; negative thinking sabotages sexual response. Be adventurous, insert a finger vaginally, wiggle it around, remove and inhale in your special bouquet. How's that for being scent-ual?

THE SWEET SMELL OF SEX-CESS

- ♥ In shower or bath, gently fold back clitoral hood and labia lips.
- ♥ Wash area with non-irritating soap; rinse thoroughly with H_2O.
- ♥ Give your sexy spots extra TLC during menstruation or if troubled with vaginitis.
- ♥ When on the go, use moist towelettes.
- ♥ That's it . . . no big deal. You've got the situation licked! (How's that for tongue in chick!)

Do Yourself a Flavor

Still with me as I'm trying to present these sensitive subjects in an informative and *tasteful* way? Which brings up the subject of **taste** . . . of an intimate kind. Feminine flavor is difficult to describe. Like other bodily functions, it changes cyclically, is affected by general and genital health and reacts to what's recently been ingested. If in good health, the taste isn't unpleasant and, in fact, could be v-e-r-y i-n-t-e-r-e-s-t-i-n-g. Curious? Well then, while no one's looking, dip in and take a taste test. Here's the scoop: While I can't promise ordinary flavors, you might luck out with sextraordinary delights such as Raunchy Road, Fraulines and Cream or Very Merry Cherry. Pleaaase . . . hold the sprinkles!

Summary of Executive Decisions

By staying motivated, playful and making regular "deposits," your orgasmic quotients are sure to escalate. On this note, let's hear from the boys in the oval orifice.

Setting a Precedent for Vaginal Orgasms

"I've BEN meaning to explain to you how greatly you'll profit from self-penetration. Remember, save your $$$ not orgasms for a zany day."

"Don't be a smart ALEX and cause internal problems using petroleum or mineral oil products. Make a safe, healthier choice with water-soluble K-Y or a lubricant such as Astro Glide."

"Honest, you owe it to yourself to keep those juices flowing with frequent self-stimulation and penetration. If I'm ABE, you're able!"

"ANDY'S handy-dandy tip: Add penetration to masturbation and up your chances of being orgasmic through intercourse."

"Barely 30% of women can climax solely through intercourse. That includes Betsy, Martha and ah, humm *you*, too? If you invest time to learn how, by GEORGE, I think you'll get it."

"I GRANT you, regular climactic contractions and/or kegeling will keep your vagina tightened, toned and feeling like a million bucks."

You Owe It to Yourself

Whether a joint or individual depositor, the bottom line is that you've learned non-taxing ways to diversify your portfolio. It's a good bet that adding self- penetration to clitoral stimulation ups your odds of becoming vaginally orgasmic, with or without a partner. Even if another *audit* is required, persevere. Then when the tax man or someone significant *cummith*, the interlude will be mutually rewarding. The *Lay Back and Do It* branch of the I.R.S. offers knowledge which enables you to gain a lifetime of orgasms. Here's an encouraging incentive:

LAY BACK AND DO IT CORP.
LOVERS LANE
YOUR PLACE, U.S.A.

DATE _____

PLAY TO THE ORDER OF: _____
(SIGN YOUR NAME HERE)

___ $1,000,000. WORTH OF ORGASM$ ___

MEMO: JUST DO IT NOW!   G.I. LOVETT

You're a winner!

5

PC— Your Magic Muscle

PC-ing Is Believing

Do you believe in magic? If you're like me, seeing is believing. For more years than I'd care to admit, I assumed I was having the world's greatest orgasms, solo and shared. Being somewhat of a *newcomer* to orgasmic pleasure (after all those years of faking *it*), you can understand my wanting to attend a workshop where the speaker digressed about a "magic" muscle that increased orgasmic intensity. Magic-schmagic! How could my sexual enjoyment get any better than it already was? The speaker explained this particular muscle was the one used to stop urination. Not exactly sexy. I did, however, recall times when I would squeeze "in there" to hug my partner's penis. He loved it, although it didn't do a heck-of-a-lot for me. After learning about the PC and how it muscled up my sexual satisfaction, I'm eager to share the inside

> **mag•ic** (maj'ik) *n.* the art or skill of performing tricks or causing startling effects. (*Feeling* is believing.)
>
> **ma•gi•cian** (me jish en) *n.* one skilled in magic. (*You* after following these instructions.)
>
> **pre•dic•tion** (pri dik shen) *n.* a foretelling of what one believes will happen. (With practice, I foresee *phenomenal orgasms* in your future.)

secret with you. Now without illusions or delusions, let's get this magic show on the road.

Now You See It

Before uncovering your PC, let's dispense with the technical jargon. Its proper name is *pubococcygeus*—read my lips, "pew-bo-cox-oh-gee-us." This band of muscle circles the vagina from pubic bone to tailbone and incredibly keeps our internal organs from sagging . . . and our sex life from dragging, if we understand its potential.

R$_x$ for Pleasure

Until 1952, the PC never gained national attention unless gynecological surgery was needed. Enter Dr. Arnold Kegel, who began prescribing PC strengthening exercises to his female patients with urinary problems. Following the doctor's suggestions, most women's medical condition improved and, wonders of wonders, flexing had surprisingly sexy side effects—some experienced orgasm for the first time and many orgasmic women became multi-orgasmic.

These medical findings were documented, but the sexual aspect didn't go public . . . or *pubic* until the seventies.

Poof! An Orgasm Appears

How, you ask, can a stronger PC increase sexual sensations? The secret's stashed deep within Pandora's box (and your's too). If this muscle is slack, an inserted finger, dildo or penis barely makes contact with the vaginal wall. If, however, the PC is taut (and taught to), whatever's inserted rubs against the wall and could conjure up spellbinding responses. Miraculously, the clitoris, vagina and anus get in on the act and poof—cataclysmic reflexes are up for grabs. Ahhh, but here's the catch.

Wimpy to Wonder-full

Facts demonstrate that two out of three women blossom into sexual maturity with a wimpy PC. Muscle strength bears no relationship to overall physical fitness. An Olympic winner could have a weaker PC than a sedentary female, or the opposite may hold true. You should opt to keep yours in shape for health reasons especially if you . . .

- ❤ Spring a leak when sneezing, laughing or exercising.
- ❤ Can't quite make it to the bathroom without leaving a telltale tinkle trail.
- ❤ Notice a decline in sexual response since giving birth.
- ❤ Feel little during self- or partner penetration and assume a larger finger dildo or penis would fill the gap.
- ❤ Have orgasms that bleep out instead of blasting off . . . that is, if you're lucky enough to climax.

Abracadabra—The PC Appears

Here's how to find your magic muscle. Since the PC controls urination, head for the bathroom and sit spread-eagle on the toilet. Start urinating then squeeze hard to stop the flow. There, you've just contracted your PC. Practice starting and stopping the flow until finished.

Presto, Change-O

You've located your PC, but in order to make it perform its erotic enchantment, it needs regular exercise. Lest this turns you off, know that flexing is simpler than pulling a rabbit out of a hat. Create some *hanky-panky* with the following:

FLEXERCISES

1. Contract the PC squeezing tightly. Don't involve the anal muscle. Breathe deeply, hold for three counts, relax your PC and exhale fully.

2. Breathe in, contracting the muscle and pulling it upward. Combine visualization with isolation. Picture a priceless object being hoisted slowly and carefully up into your vagina—for instance, a strand of precious pearls, the key to a brand new Ferrari on a gold chain, a string of winning lotto tickets. Get the idea?

3. If the muscle begins trembling, start with mini PC squeezes instead of one biggie.

4. Hopefully, you're still stringing along. Okay, now clench, release then rapidly flutter your PC.

Don't kick the kegel habit. Flex twice daily until twenty or more can easily be completed.

How to Get a Good Grip in Yourself

Here's a little slight of hand or finger, to be exact, that puts you in touch with your magic muscle.

GET IN TOUCH WITH YOUR PC

1. Lie down and insert your finger about one inch into the vagina. Notice the inner wall is smooth, however, the firm part is your PC.

2. Rotate your finger and get acquainted with its defined ridges.

3. Clench the muscle around your finger, drawing it upwards. Release and repeat.

4. Give your finger the hardest hug possible squeezing it up, up, up, holding for 10 counts.

5. Reverse gears and bear down fully. Attempt to push your finger out of the vagina without involving the anal muscle. Relax and repeat.

Astonishingly, the PC strengthens quickly, and after only a few short weeks of faithful flexing you'll notice the special orgasmic effects while masturbating or making love. More good news: flexing is ageless—it's never too early or late to start. Naturally, the sooner begun the quicker the benefits. To prevent your magic muscle and outrageous orgasms from doing a disappearing act, continue Kegeling throughout life.

Who Knows Where or When

You can sneakily flex your PC anywhere, anytime, with no one the wiser— while waiting for a bus, a big Mac, or maybe Mac himself. I'm an avid tennis player and wish my game was in as good shape as my PC. Believe it or not, I flex while waiting for my opponent to serve 'em up. On the court, I may not give Martina or Stephie a run for it, but off the court my PC might just beat the competition. Kegel anyone?

Stop Being Wishy Washy

After flexing regularly, the majority of women report being able to attain stronger, longer orgasms. Jennifer T. describes her PC experience below.

JENNIFER . . . PC PEFORMER

"When I'm on the edge of an orgasm, I focus in on my PC. Then as I climax, I'll keep flexing to lengthen and strengthen contractions. As orgasm subsides, I flex a few times for good measure. Doing this has actually increased the intensity and doubled the contractions.

Before becoming a PC performer, barely half a dozen wishy-washy contractions bleeped out. Sure they felt great but now . . . **wow**! Since keeping count, my magic number has increased to sweet sixteen and I'm having too much fun to quit trying for more."

Create Your Own Magic

Eureka! Without being a magician, **you** can create outrageous orgasms. Isn't it good to know you needn't wait for someone to mastermind your sex life. Harold, Hank or Houdini *ain't* gonna make it happen. With knowledge, power and persistance, magic will flourish.

I'll PC-ing YOU!

G-Spot— Gush-Oh "G"

Weathering a Storm of Controversy

Sexual Forecast: *Intense heat and a possibility of showers*

For years, a sexual phenomenon has caused a storm of controversy. Mother Nature's storms are named. This one, of a sexual nature, is called the G-spot in recognition of Dr. Ernst Grafenberg, who in 1944 first located and described this controversial erogenous zone. It took nearly forty years for the climate to change until medical and sexual professionals acknowledged that some females could ejaculate from G-spot stimulation. Before you throw cold water on this theory, read how yours truly got into the swim of things.

The G and Me

My own non-medical, living-proof theory is unless you've experienced a G-spot climax you won't be a believer. I have—I swear on a stack of vibrators! What I'm about to relate isn't the wild fabrication of a sex-crazed writer, it's the truth, the whole truth, and . . .

The Fickle Finger of Dr. Dan D.

I can't remember the exact day I had my first G-spot orgasm but it happened while dating a newly graduated Med. student. Dr. Dan was a practical joker and a playful lover on top of it all. One night he knocked on my door and said, "The doctor is here to see you now." He dressed for the occasion: stethoscope, white jacket, rubber gloves . . . that's all. After a quick external (a.k.a. foreplay), he donned a rubber glove, lubricated his finger of choice and got down, or rather **up**, to business. Instead of telling me to assume the usual embarrassing gynecological position, Dan directed me to remain standing. Acting semi-professional, the good doctor started my pelvic exam. He caught me by surprise when he curved his inserted finger and moved it rhythmically back and forth. As the examination continued, I went into orbit and, within minutes, maybe seconds, experienced a most incredible orgasm. Wave after wave of pleasure melted me as I melted in his arms.

The Game Continues in Spite of Rain

We proceeded onto the examining table (otherwise known as the bed) and **it** happened again, only this time I spurted a huge gush. This strange feeling plus the huge outpouring made me think I'd wet the bed. Embarrassed as I was, it felt too good to stop and I floated enthusiastically toward a soggy round #2, then #3. The sheets were soaked when we finally collapsed in exhaustion, falling contentedly asleep on a gigantic wet spot.

Getting Off on Rubber

On the next house call, the good doctor explained what had occurred. He said I was having G-spot orgasms and suggested we put towels down on the bed. I followed doctor's orders, but even king-sized ones didn't soak up the evidence, so off I went to Bloomie's baby department to buy a rubber sheet. The salesgirl politely inquired as to how old my baby was and looked astonished when I laughingly replied "in her thirties." Little did she suspect it was me getting off on rubber. Dandy Dan even showed me how to find the G-spot for myself. To this day, I'm grateful for his assistance in helping me discover this delightful phenomenon which I want to share with you now.

 ## Where the Heck Is It Anyway?

Although all women have a G-spot, most don't know where this fountain of pleasure is hiding out. It's found two to three inches in along the front of the vaginal wall, nestled between the pubic bone and cervix. Continuously probed, this hot spot can react cataclysmically like the clitoris with one wondrous difference: it's capable of triggering vaginal orgasms resulting in spurting fluid. The spot is actually a collection of small erectile tissue composed of ultra-sensitive nerves. During arousal it may swell to the size of a dime and become larger than a quarter (how's that for in-flation). G-spots vary, as do breasts and penises, but size isn't indicative of capacity to generate satisfaction.

Different Types of Orgasms? ___ *True* ___ *False*

A test was devised so that sex researchers could evaluate whether women could experience different orgasms. Two methods of measuring response were used: one monitored the orgasmic platform (or PC muscle), another recorded muscular activity within the vagina. Researchers could then discern which area stirred up the biggest storm.*

This proved that some women do experience different orgasms. Women who have enjoyed both climaxes claim uterine orgasms are deeper and often more quickly attained; however, once G-spot orgasm is experienced, it enables women to more

> ### *THE VERDICT
> * Direct clitoral stimulation produces stronger contractions.
> * G-spot arousal generates more intense uterine muscle reflexes that can unleash torrents of love juice.

easily achieve multiple climaxes. This brings females as much satisfaction as ejaculation does to men—maybe more, as these wet 'n wild cloudbursts can continue.

Up the Bladder to Success

Because of its proximity to the urethra, hunting for the elusive G-spot creates the bothersome need to urinate. That's why it's important to empty your bladder before G-spot prodding. Only then will you be able to ignore the feeling of urgency and fully get into sexual sensations. During this critical phase of stimulation you must allow your body to fully relax and be enveloped by the overwhelming feelings. Pulling out sexual stoppers and maintaining a devil-may-care sense of abandonment is what leads to liquid orgasm.

What Is This Thing Called Love Juice?

G-spot liquid contains chemical ingredients similar to male ejaculate minus, of course, sperm. Unlike semen or urine, the fluid is watery, clear and fragrant-free. If, however, *ur-ine* doubt, check it out! Inquisitive enough for the taste test? You'll find it bland. Not Haegen Daz, but totally fat-free!

How Much *Cummeth*?

The Tennessee Valley, Grand Coolie, Hoover—frankly, my dear, who gives a *dam* how much "cummeth"? I've heard amounts ranging from a teaspoon to a cupful and guess I float somewhere in the middle. Quality not quantity is the issue here so don't hold back.

G-Whiz, Just Relax

G-spot climax or lack of it is no criterion for sexual satisfaction. Some women simply need to develop muscle control to have deep orgasms (refer to the section on PC exercises, Chapter 5), while others may not have a desire to experiment with their G-spot. Whatever the reason, don't put a damper on your adventurous spirit. If it works, great. If not, have fun with your other erogenous zones. In other words, if the first time you have a dry run, try, try again.

"G" Marks the Spot

Let's summarize how to get your finger on the pulse of this pleasure center.

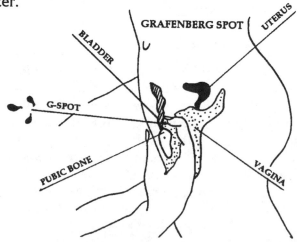

1. Empty your bladder. I know, I know, not exactly a romantic start, but remember, your first sensation will be the need to potty . . . not party!

2. Place your middle finger into your vagina and slowly pass the bumpy surface along the vaginal wall. Slide your finger in until it contacts the cervix. Notice how silky smooth the surface is, much like the head of a penis, ummm. R-E-L-A-X and proceed slowly. Remember you're searching for buried treasure that affords you rich rewards.

3. Bring your finger back down to the vaginal entrance. Now curve it and start in again. Move straight up the vaginal wall, tap, tap, tapping against the pubic bone as you go. After proceeding an inch or two inside and slightly right or left of center, you'll feel a small jolt and the need to urinate. Congratulations, you've struck gold!

4. Continue rhythmically massaging the area with gentle yet firm pressure. You must **get past the uncomfortable feeling** of needing to urinate. Erase everything else from your mind and visualize your body exploding in ecstasy. If drops of urine escape, don't panic, that's what the towel is for.

5. Steadily apply firm-to-strong prodding until the need to "tinkle" is replaced by a deep sensual feeling, unlike clitoral arousal. By now your spot is beginning to swell . . . and feels swell, too.

THE BEST POSITIONS

(*Don't forget to put the towel under you.*)
- Sit on a chair. Bend forward and spread your legs wide apart . . . *or*
- Get on your knees. Keeping your derrière in the air, bend down with your head resting on a pillow.

THE WORST POSITION

Don't lie on your back. Gravity pulls the organs down and away from the vaginal entrance, so you'd need either a **very short vagina** or **extra l-o-n-g fingers** to reach the area.

6. For added intensity get both hands in on the action. While one is busy **inside** fiddling with your G-spot, use the other hand to apply downward pressure on the **outside** of your abdomen, just above the pubic bone.

7. If you get lucky, don't stop after the first gush. Let yourself go with the flow and ride the rapturous waves as long as you can.

Throwing a Curve

Even having a partner can't guarantee G-spot orgasms, unless he uses his finger, or is one of the few men who sports a curved penis. Without the bend, "doggie-style" entry may be the way to have a G-spot climax during intercourse. In other words, minus the curve, it's difficult for the real McCoy or substitute toy to hit the mark. **When you become G-spot smart, you'll be able to direct your finger, his penis or whatever, whenever you're ready to take the pleasure plunge**.

Gee, This Hits the Spot

Now that the G-spot has been summarized, localized and idolized, let's get it energized. Since these unique orgasms can add immeasurably to your sexual interludes, don't get discouraged before turning on with a toy designed especially for G-spot joy. To make for smoother sailing, lubricate your plaything with water-soluble surgical gel such as K-Y.

G-spot Sleeve

This nubby, curved latex sleeve slips onto a seven-inch battery-operated dildo.

G-spotter Attachment

This smooth vinyl four-inch- by one-inch-attachment is made to fit over the **Magic Wind** by Hitachi. Slim enough to slip into the snuggest places, it's curved to superbly stimulate *that* spot.

G-spotter Plus

This sleeve is four inches long and one inch in diameter; it pops atop most multi-attachment electric vibrators.

Wiggle Stick or Flex-a-Pleaser

This battery-powered, flexible, ultraslim, long-handled toy transmits variable speed vibrations. Its curved head is angled to glide easily across your trigger point.

How Are Conditions in Your Area?

"Weather" experiencing a climate of showers or undergoing a dry spell, nothing need dampen your pursuit of G-spot gratification. Not successful today? Keep pluggin' on as conditions can change rapidly. Either way, don't let it cloud your erotic enjoyment as you soak up super sexuality, solo or shared.

FEMALE FIREWORKS

Perineum— A Little-Known Hot Spot

The Princess and the "P"

Just when you thought you had a finger, fun thing or friend on the pulse of your hot spots, maybe there's one you missed. Both sexes have this surprisingly sensuous site, but most don't have a clue to its location. Often those in the know rarely give it the TLC it so readily responds to. As a result, this erogenous zone is often overlooked and underplayed.

E.S.P. = Extra-Sensitive Perineum

What and where is it? I thought you'd never ask! Called the **perineum**, all two inches or so of this petite pleasure playground sits centered between two goal posts—the vagina and anus. These three titillating treasures share the same sensitive tissue, causing anything introduced vaginally or analy to stimulate the perineum.

Some Nerve

The easiest way to find yours is by sexy flexing. Give it a try while reading this. Simply squeeze your PC muscle hard, release then repeat. If you don't feel tugging with every tightening, then get to work on developing this potential pleaser. Check further by placing a finger on the perineum or bend over and hang a look; you'll see it moving as you flex. Integrate flexing with things done on a daily basis such as brushing your teeth, driving or waiting in line at the bank.

Touchy Stimulation

Use a finger to explore the effects of perineum touching. It should feel stimulating unless you've recently given birth and had an episiotomy. In this case, there may be tenderness or numbness (which may subside in time). That reminds me, I first learned about the perineum during pregnancy. My female OB/GYN encouraged her patients to massage their perineum during the final months. This promotes circulation and decreases the need for sutures after delivery, besides . . . it feels good. So listen to the doctor, whether preggie or not.

Perennial Flower Power

To recline is divine, but not when targeting your perineum. Instead, sit comfortably with knees bent and feet flat on the bed or floor. Keep your legs spread and push your pelvis forward. As you cultivate your perennial Garden of Eden, ecstasy will blossom.

Winning Ways

To get your perineum perking, start by stroking your inner thighs and lightly pass over perineum with the backs of your fingers. If your nails are long, flick them back and forth barely grazing the sensitive skin. Playfully "paint" figure eights, or toss in some lotto numbers. This is the winning ticket to develop perineum *response-ability* for added sexual joy, solo or shared.

Improve Your Smile

Using a new, soft pediatric toothbrush, lightly stroke perineum up to the vaginal entrance then glide lightly around the opening. Now run the bristles away then back again. After getting sufficiently revved up, insert brush **no further** than an inch or two and gently swirl around. Sounds silly, you say? Don't give this idea the brush off 'til giving it a try.

Right to the Point

Using a long-handled sable art brush, roll the bristles into a point before dipping tip in warm oil. Now "paint" a mini masterpiece on your hot little perineum canvas. Equally effective are cosmetic and narrow sponge brushes.

This 'n That

Bring into play other enjoyable items such as feathers, artificial silk flowers, strands of beads or a hand-shaped back scratcher. Use them to tickle, tap, tease, scratch, brush and flick along the pleasing pathway.

> **REMEMBER**
>
> Nothing sharp, splintery, breakable or unsanitary should ever be used inside, outside, or rubbed from back to front.

Pick-a-Dilly

Hold a smooth battery-powered plastic dildo at different angles, moving it teasingly along the perineum for a few minutes before inserting vaginally. Experiment with a *Flex-a-Pleaser,* which has a long handle and curved, smooth, plastic vibrating head.

Most stimulating is an electric multi-attachment vibrator, using its long, narrow tip or ball-shaped snap-on accessories.

Note: Toys can be propped in place with a pillow. This hands-free method allows you to tug simultaneously on labial lips. Since these sensitive nerves are all interconnected, you'll get a double whammy. I promise, your perineum will respond happily.

A Man's Point of View

While writing this chapter, I asked my friend Steve (a.k.a. "Stud Muffin") if he knew what the perineum was. Laughingly, he replied, "Sure do, I use it for a chin rest!"

Clitoris—
Out-of-This-World
Pleasure

Dream Lovers

Wouldn't you love to . . . "Discover the mysteries of your destiny," "Explore the fate of your love relationships," "Know you'll never have to fake another orgasm again"? Madame Rozella can gaze into her crystal ball and predict you'll find a special soul mate but, realistically speaking, it's your orgasmic energy and accompanying responses that will keep you eternally satisfied. Your ability to have heightened erotic encounters is attainable, and there's no time like the present to create *sex-cess* . . . solo or with a dream lover.

Wish Craft

 Astrologists, palmists and psychics might grudgingly agree that their predictions hold little power. It's your own beliefs and attitude, not gypsy bugaboo, which determine the outcome of your experiences. Past choices influence what's presently occurring. To verify this, let's evaluate your sexual evolution. Have you . . .

★ Felt "inclined" for sex but fallen asleep instead?

★ Faked **it** so much you've no idea how to fix the predicament?

* Seen the sun set 50, 1,000, 10,000 times since your last orgasm?

* Blamed some unmagical "prince" for being a lousy lover and not giving you the orgasms you deserve?

The truth is the universe has wondrously supplied **all** women with a supernatural hot spot guaranteed to turn their sex life from vague into Venus. If you're not getting spellbinding orgasms, it could be because 1) you don't think you deserve to or 2) you're unsure how to make it happen.

The solution is simple and simply spectacular:

* Decide to change now.

* Learn how to *make love to, for and with yourself.*

* Turn sexual energy on and on and on and **world-class orgasms** will come (pun intended).

It's no mystery. The ability to climax is a natural reaction and by exciting your nerve pathways response magically flourishes. Master the following techniques, stay on course with a personal commitment to change and almost immediately your sexual future will make astonishing advances.

Keys and Clues from Past Lives

What is this mystical zone of passion all women possess? Centuries ago the Greeks named **it** *Kleitoris,* derived from the root word *Kleis* meaning "key." Imagine, wise men correctly named this direct route to unlocking women's sexuality well before the English language was formed! Still the issue over this bedazzling bud of erogenous tissue remains Greek to most men . . . and *women*— a puzzling phenomenon to be sure!

U.F.O.s = Unlimited Fabulous Orgasms

The epi-center of a woman's sexual cosmos is da-da-da-DAT-DA-DA . . . the **clitoris!**

It's the only organ in the body existing exclusively for sexual arousal. The clitoris is the birthplace of orgasmic delight and the cradle of erotica. Mother Nature is extremely generous. There's no limit to the amount of climaxes this fervent little spellbinder can bestow. Fortunately, unlike the male counterpart, we needn't wait for erection or resurrection either . . . a decided advantage over the penis! That wizardess of female form engineered us perfectly. We can navigate our heavenly bodies to ecstasy ***whenever we choose***. What a concept!

Threshold of Magical Sex-citement

The clitoris is so out-of-this-world sexy that with proper stimulation a whopping 98% of females are orgasmically responsive. In *The Hite Report,* Shere Hite stated, "70% of women needed adequate clitoral stimulation to orgasm during intercourse." During masturbation, a climax can occur within minutes. Through penetration alone, it may take hours, days or decades! Understandably, few partners are able or willing to devote this much time, causing countless women to fake orgasm attempting to bolster the male ego and solidify their relationship.

By continuing to fake orgasm and not taking responsibility for our own satisfaction, the problem is perpetuated. We can't blame our partners for not bringing us to climax. Possibly no one taught them or us . . . that is, until now!

The Male Myth:
"Real women orgasm by intercourse alone."

Extra Terrestrial Teasers

In truth, the majority of men would give the earth, moon and stars to satisfy their love goddesses in bed. In fact, their self-image of being the world's greatest lovers may depend on it. Men aren't alien to pleasing us sexually. Many unfortunately believe staying power is the secret: "If I can last l-o-n-g e-n-o-u-g-h, she's gonna climax" . . . not true! You probably require more clitoral caressing along with some info on what's happening down there.

Love Match—The Clitoris vs. the Penis

The clitoris is a female version of his "member in good standing," not a pint-sized edition. This petite powerhouse lends credence to the theory that size has nothing to do with *sighs*. Externally, man's best friend (the penis) appears larger. Incredulously, however, the clitoral root and corresponding internal structures

Vulva: Clitoris, labial lips, urethra and vaginal opening.

Clitoral Root: Attached to pubic pone by a band of connective tissue is the highly reactive clitoral root or shaft. It divides like a wishbone into two sections, spreading dreamy pleasure over a wide area.

Labia Major: Larger outer lips that sweetly and discretely shelter vaginal area.

Clitoris Glans (or Tip): A tiny treasure of exploding pleasure about the size of a small pearl.

Vestibule: Tissue that surrounds the clitoral shaft. Much like a penis, it swells during sexual arousal creating the desire to explode into ecstasy.

Clitoral Hood: Soft fold of skin protecting clitoris. At orgasm the supersensitive clitoral tip retracts and temporarily hides under its sheath.

Labia Minor: Inner lips which moisten the intimate entrance with a nectar called sebum.

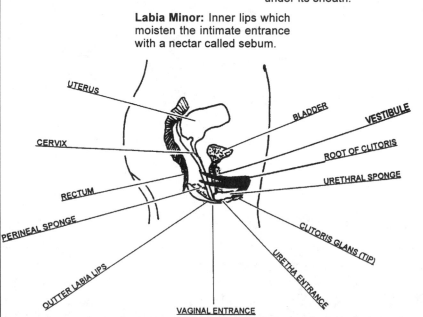

UTERUS

CERVIX

RECTUM

PERINEAL SPONGE

OUTTER LABIA LIPS

BLADDER

VESTIBULE

ROOT OF CLITORIS

URETHRAL SPONGE

CLITORIS GLANS (TIP)

URETHA ENTRANCE

VAGINAL ENTRANCE

may be a sizable match to his romantic rover. Is the exact location of your clitoris still a mystery? Gaze upon its whereabouts:

Heavens to Betsy, Betty and Bea

The most predictable way to become orgasmic is through solo experimentation. Novices to masturbation seeking instant gratification usually head straight for the tender clitoral head. This mega physical mistake results in an "Ouch!" instead of an "Aaah." If this disappointing experience has happened to you, take heart, you're like most of us; it's just not a subject women talk about to each other or with a man. Jump in and see how Joy, a computer analyst from New Jersey, reacts to direct clitoral contact.

FICKLE FINGER OF SEX-CESS

"Many times during intimacy with a new partner I start getting heavenly feelings when, *wham-o*, he'll squeeze, not please, my clitoris. What a bummer! I come down from my sexual high as if I were pushed off a mountain. The hairs on my body stand straight up, and it takes several minutes to regain my composure. After going through this numerous times, I had enough. Now I select a choice finger and guide it around, not on, my clitoris. You can bet this gets me jumping for joy!"

Fascinating Journey

Aladdin rubbing his magic lamp, or other priceless treasure, can't derive more joy than you after treating yourself to an exquisite excursion.

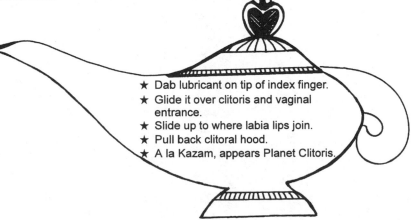

★ Dab lubricant on tip of index finger.
★ Glide it over clitoris and vaginal entrance.
★ Slide up to where labia lips join.
★ Pull back clitoral hood.
★ A la Kazam, appears Planet Clitoris.

WIZEN UP

Self-pleasuring is as natural and normal as breathing. If preposterous outdated zappers about touching your genitals keeps you from doing these *seXercises*, don a pair of soft, surgical rubber gloves or use a vibrator. In no time at all, you'll toss the gloves (although I'm sure you'll keep the vibe).

While performing this magical maneuvering, keep in mind every earthly goddess responds uniquely. A right-handed woman may find the left side of her clitoral shaft unresponsive, while the right side sends her in orbit (or vice versa). Like the galaxies, there are endless arousing possibilities to discover with your heavenly body. Enjoy the quest leaving no zone unexplored.

Star-Studded Techniques

Prepare to embark on a quest of inner and outer fulfillment. Are all systems fired up and ready for blast off?

CHECK THE FOLLOWING

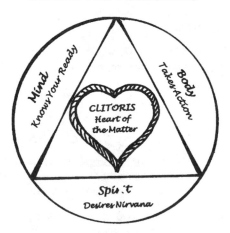

Journey to where no man may have gone before . . . (sure, sure).

Now, maintain a sense of abandonment and succumb to lusty feelings. When you find a particular movement that jettisons you to another world, **stay with it**. An orgasm may be waiting in the wings. Add enthusiasm and creativity to the following techniques and away you go. The sky (not the guy) is the limit.

★ Stroke area from pubes to perineum, using index finger.

★ Focus in on the heavenly feeling radiating throughout your clitoris.

★ Sense wetness developing within your vagina.

★ Dip a finger in and spread moisture along labia.

★ Playfully proceed to teasingly orbit the miniature . . .

THE SKY'S THE LIMIT

★ Part labial lips and slide back clitoral hood.

★ Travel to the fifth dimension by planting feet against headboard or wall. Repeat maneuvers, aiming for new heights of satisfaction.

★ Take a handful of pubic hair, playfully tug then release.

★ Exert pressure on pubes using palm of hand while brushing fingers across clitoral hood.

★ Separate outer lips then, using thumb, gently strum inner ones.

★ Lie tummy down across a pillow and massage mons. Hug, tug, rotate then release. Stimulate entire mons area with circular movements. Press, release, go up and down, at various speeds.

★ Run a finger up and down either side of clitoris, teasing around, not directly on its tender tip.

Before returning to earth, linger on cloud nine and revel in the rapturous feelings just experienced. If you haven't yet gotten in touch with an orgasm, don't despair—the adventure continues accompanied by some oout-of-this-world accouterments. Read how Grace psyched herself up sexually.

AMAZING . . . GRACE

I never dreamed joining a singles club would be my thing, but finding suitable dates had become a problem that warranted a solution. While scanning the newspapers, I came across an ad for a psychic fair which read: **"Learn the Secrets to Happiness and Lasting Relationships!"** I flew out the door and within an hour was seated in front of Lady Sabrina and her deck of tarot cards. She looked the picture of an old Spanish gypsy, weighted down with make-up and rings on every finger. I began questioning my sanity. Per her instructions, I handed over a piece of paper with my name written on it. She studied my signature while spreading the cards.

"Ahhhh," she softly exclaimed. "You're much too pretty to be so lonely. Let's see what your problem is. Mmm." Sounded like Lady Sabrina was on to something. She tuned into the fact that I'd previously had many suitors but felt unsatisfied in those relationships. "Fill the void within yourself and find true love," she said. Asking her to be more specific she continued. "It's amazing, Grace, that a successful, intelligent woman like yourself doesn't have self-confidence with men. You need to let self-love explode." I wondered if she was indeed psychic and knew I'd never orgasmed. Yep, that's exactly what she meant! Finished with the reading, she put her warm hand over mine, smiled and said, "For your own good, treat yourself to a wand vibrator, use it sexually to massage your magic spot and, presto, satisfaction will come." I took her advice and determinedly purchased one on my way home. She was right. Later that night I had my first orgasm ever and cried as a lifetime of frustration flowed out. Do I now believe in meta physics? I'm not certain, even though Sabrina tuned in to my physical dilemma. There's no guarantee I'll find a "soul mate," but exploring my sexuality and learning to love myself is now a top priority. Since I don't feel desperate anymore, finding "Mr. Right" isn't the critical issue it used to be . . . and what a relief!

Lady Sabrina

Redeeming Vibrations

Are you desperately seeking your "Prince" and/or an elusive orgasm? Before checking your astrological sign, cracking open a fortune cookie or trusting psychic consultation, check out the wizardry a vibrator can conjure up. If you haven't yet purchased a wand or multi-attachment massager, for heaven's sake, get shaking and go shopping (refer to Stores in Chapter 7). Here's enlightenment on a few playthings that create cosmic clitoral combustion.

Multi-Attachment Vibrator

Many women love this joy toy for clitoral stimulation. Regular variety store models are packaged with at least four winning tips. Sex shop brands have additional attachments to choose from including insertable twigs and a penis cup, for shared "good vibrations."

Wand Massager

Cast a magic spell on self-pleasure using a vibrating wand. All models offer dual speed with a massaging head about the size of a tennis (not crystal) ball. Available in super stimulating rechargeable models, they're rapidly becoming the climax-producing stimulator of choice. They easily provide inspiration and *sexcitation* when positioned between yourself and a special someone.

Mighty Mini Massager

This three-inch super nova powered by one AA battery fits easily in your purse. Be ready for many celestial trips.

Venus Butterfly

This pretty pink silicone butterfly with adjustable straps fits comfortably around your waist and thighs for hands-free stimulation. The tail titillates labia folds while the butterfly's head buzzes clitoris. (Wear during dildo, finger penetration or lovemaking and receive a double delight.)

Instant Sextasy

Take a direct route to arousal using a wand massager or multi-attachment vibe with the Love Cup tip. Think of it as a space-age vehicle to sexually take you where you want to go. Why invest lots of time and money in sessions with a psychic when you can buy either of these vibes and instantly put good fortune in the palm of your hand?

Hold everything! If this is your first time using a vibrator, start slowly. Set a mood that suits your style, r-e-l-a-x and position yourself with knees bent, legs apart. Begin by moving massager across hands, arms, breasts and belly. Criss-cross pubes and circle up down and around inner thighs. Experiment using various pressures and adjust vibe speed for comfort.

Ready? Here's how to deal yourself a winning hand and empower the passion that lies within:

1. Stroke inner thigh brushing vibe across perineum to opposite leg before drifting back to mons.

2. Lay massager on flattened fingertips then slide to clitoris and gently pull back clitoral hood.

3. Push down and circle removing hand for direct vibrator stimulation.

4. Orbit over labia, across perineum and traverse back to clitoris.

5. As merriment mounts, build excitation by continually lifting vibe away and back again.

6. Crave stronger stimulation? Roll onto belly then gyrate genitals over massager.

7. Want more? Practice *seXercises* in Vibrators, Chapter 20.

Aspire to Fly Higher

You don't have to gaze into crystal balls, read tarot cards or study the stars to create superb changes in your sex life. The truth is you already possess everything you need. Find the key to unleash your rapturous hot spot. Allow its hidden power to transform you into a highly reactive, sensual goddess. Elevate your eroticism and move in the direction of your dreams, whether journeying solo or accompanied by a planetary partner. You deserve frolicking among the stars. Enjoy the trip!

Bedroom— Create a Steamy Sanctuary

A Sensuous Bedroom? Sure, Why Not?

Although any room's a possible setting for *Sizzlin' Sex*, can you think of a better place than milady's boudoir? Since most encounters of a sexual kind (solo or shared) are likely to occur in the bedroom, why not create an especially inviting environment? It will make a delightful difference to you and anyone you invite in.

Your private paradise should be a place where you shed cares along with clothes—a serene yet raunchy retreat where you can revel in restful Zzz's as well as X-rated romping. It's hard to believe we spend twelve hours a day in the bedroom, dressing, dreaming, napping, noshing, etc. If, like me, you're exercising and *seXercising* there too. It could be a lot more! Being such an important room, wouldn't you love it to reflect and revitalize your sensuality?

On a budget? You don't have to spend a queen's ransom unless you want snazzy new furniture. Compare it to whipping up haute cuisine without investing in a dream kitchen: Decide what ingredients whet your erotic appetite, make a list, shop for prime components, add a dash of creativity then savor the fruits of your labor of love. With inspiration from some babes and their bedtime stories, design a passion-filled playground. Let's visit Vicki and see what's cookin' and I don't mean in the kitchen!

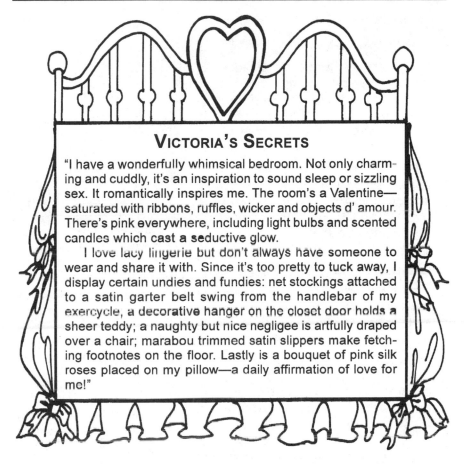

VICTORIA'S SECRETS

"I have a wonderfully whimsical bedroom. Not only charming and cuddly, it's an inspiration to sound sleep or sizzling sex. It romantically inspires me. The room's a Valentine—saturated with ribbons, ruffles, wicker and objects d' amour. There's pink everywhere, including light bulbs and scented candles which cast a seductive glow.

I love lacy lingerie but don't always have someone to wear and share it with. Since it's too pretty to tuck away, I display certain undies and fundies: net stockings attached to a satin garter belt swing from the handlebar of my exercycle; a decorative hanger on the closet door holds a sheer teddy; a naughty but nice negligee is artfully draped over a chair; marabou trimmed satin slippers make fetching footnotes on the floor. Lastly is a bouquet of pink silk roses placed on my pillow—a daily affirmation of love for me!"

Add fans, fluff and luscious, lacy essentials to inspire desire by being constantly in view. Caution: these feminine touches tug at his heart strings (and other good places, too), teasingly offering promises of fantasies to come. See a hot plot unfold during a night of solo amour or with a knight in shinning armor. Honest, this works for me and can for you, too.

Once Upon a Mattress

Although intimate interludes occur on sofas, chairs and floors, for most, of us the bed's an optimal choice. We spend approximately one-third of our lives on one, so choose your mattress carefully with more than sleep in mind. Here's a bedroom blooper from Betty.

ONCE UPON A MATTRESS

"I'm a busy gal who truly treasures private evenings curled up in bed. When It came time to shop for a new mattress, I wanted it perfect in everyway . . . like the lover I'd been fantasizing about.

Headboard: It had to have 1) a place to store sexy toys, 2) built-in illumination (to throw light on any subject) and 3) be attractive. . . like my pretend partner.

Mattress: As with men, I prefer one that is hard, firm enough for fun, minus lumps 'n bumps.

Frame: I wanted it strong and solid, able to shake, rattle 'n roll without disturbing neighbors.

I was pleased with my selection until meeting the man of my dreams. It then became a nightmare as the mattress was too short for him!"

— *Betty*

As Betty illustrates, one size may not fit all. Choose a mattress long enough to fit the area without overcrowding, then pick your roommate accordingly.

Motion à la Emotion

Wanna buy something delightfully different? Dive in and explore the pleasures of Neptune's nocturne in a waterbed. You say I'm all wet because you get seasick? Hold it, you won't need Dramamine® or a sailor for a sidekick. Newer styles are virtually motionless, hug the body yet feel warm and cozy. What's more, even minus a mate, you'll receive a massage via an optional built-in vibrator. Using your favorite adult toy along with the massager, you'll raise *Cain* but never *mutiny*. Another reason people avoided waterbeds was that they were difficult to climb out of. Jell sides eliminate the problem. Live in a cold climate? The bed's heater helps keep the room toasty and eliminates frigid romps on cold sheets, brrr! An award-winning feature that's never advertised is waterbeds are easy on the knees and give way to love-hungry heavyweights, as Patty portrays.

ANCHORS A-WEIGH

"My husband's so large that he's nicknamed Porky. Truthfully, I'm not so slender, but if Porky sat on a cow he'd make instant hamburger patties! His weight was causing some huge sexual problems. He was too wide for me to straddle and his majigger wasn't long enough for side-by-side penetration. While doing it in bed, we always ended up with Porky on top, me being crushed below and his knees suffering from sheet burn! Luckily, a friend suggested trying a waterbed. It's saved me from suffocation, our sex life's improved and Porky feels a heck of a lot better without those sore knees."

— *Patty*

Move 'R and Shake Her

Motorized beds with their different positions can be advantageously adapted to auto-eroticism. Those with built-in massagers create a stir in any angle. One manufacturer states: "By simply flicking a switch, you receive pulsating energy simulating the gentle fingers of a skilled masseur." Understandably, many people find these vibrating sensations blissfully stimulating. Lori has an interesting story to share.

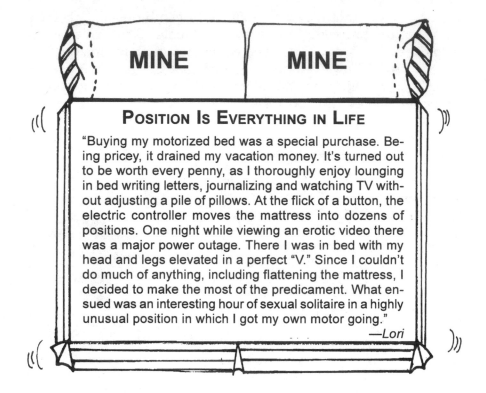

POSITION IS EVERYTHING IN LIFE

"Buying my motorized bed was a special purchase. Being pricey, it drained my vacation money. It's turned out to be worth every penny, as I thoroughly enjoy lounging in bed writing letters, journalizing and watching TV without adjusting a pile of pillows. At the flick of a button, the electric controller moves the mattress into dozens of positions. One night while viewing an erotic video there was a major power outage. There I was in bed with my head and legs elevated in a perfect "V." Since I couldn't do much of anything, including flattening the mattress, I decided to make the most of the predicament. What ensued was an interesting hour of sexual solitaire in a highly unusual position in which I got my own motor going."

—*Lori*

My Pad—Not Yours

A mattress pad's a good idea for any bed, especially when using oils, lotions or other fun stuff that might seep through the sheet. Using two pads keeps wet spots from wandering and leaving telltale signs on the mattress.

Ah, Sheet

Some women find satin sheets seductive. Although these look sexy, they get icy cold in winter then stick to skin when body temperature rises. Forget them all together if using oils which leave stains in fabric. I save satin for lingerie which comes off before love lubes go on.

Spread the Word

You don't need the high-priced spread to add crowning glory to the queen's quarters. Jazz up a plain one as Susan did:

SPREADING ROMANCE

"I searched high and low for the perfect bedspread. Something different, not too busy. The pursuit ended with a beautiful bargain: a thick, luxurious, off-white comforter. Since it looked lovely but blah, I trimmed the edges with lace then imagined a big pink heart in the center. Why not paint one on, I thought? Using fabric paints and brush, within minutes, the masterpiece was finished. A lovely pink heart now adorns my comforter. Still inspired, I painted matching pillow shams, tied on ribbons and the compliments haven't stopped. Don't be discouraged; I'm no artist, so you can do it, too! My boyfriend teases me by saying, 'I have the biggest *heart-on* he's ever seen.' Bet you saw that coming!"

—*Susan*

On the Lighter Side

When creating an atmosphere for erotic enhancement, the importance of lustrous lighting is often overlooked. Why be left in the dark when something simple as a pale pink bulb or flickering candle makes a substantial difference? Movie makers pay paramount attention to proper lighting and so should women wanting to add intimate touches. Achieve stunning star quality in your boudoir with these illuminating suggestions:

- Flatter your body with soft-colored bulbs that com-plement skin tone.
- Light liquid or scented candles and place in front of mirror. Flickers hide lumps, bumps or other bothersome stuff, teasingly hinting of what's coming off.
- Lay a small fluorescent light fixture on the floor behind bed or dresser.

- Install track or similar accent lighting over bed with a dimmer control.
- Small plug-in spot or night lights create soft lighting.
- Natural sunlight streaming through decorative wood-en shutters allows seductive shadows to play upon your body.
- True love may be blind but the neighbors aren't. When the action's horizontal, vertical blinds come to the rescue. These panels adjust to let in light yet keep action out of sight.

If neighbors are close and privacy's a priority, consider covering windows with metallic tint. During daytime it lets in the view while shielding you. When the sun sets and lights are lit, tint vanishes so cover windows as usual. Sneak a peek at what happened to Sadie from Sarasota:

SADIE, THE NOT SO SHADY LADY

"At the time we installed solar window tinting, our thought was lowering cooling costs. I never dreamt this would raise my internal temperature. The windows became semi-reflective outside which makes it impossible to peek in without pressing your nose to the glass. After installation, I felt comfortable undressing without drawing the shades. One day our handsome yardman was mowing the lawn. Watching his muscular body ripple in the sun made my old loins lusty. I locked the bedroom door, headed back to the window and began fantasizing. Piece by piece I hesitantly undressed while touching, tickling and tweaking myself shamelessly in front of the window. With legs spread, I fondled and stimulated my 'privates' until I swooned with long-forgotten feelings. Unable to continue standing, I sank to the floor, quivering in delight. It made me laugh thinking no one will ever know the pleasure I got watching that yardman. If he only knew, he'd probably charge me double. You know what? It would be worth the price!"

Hot and Cold Running Sex

Don't you agree that being too hot or cold inhibits sex play? Efforts spent creating an alluring bedroom will be for naught if you've got to dress like Nordica of the North to keep from freezing to death. On the other hand, a room that's too hot to handle yourself in definitely dulls desires. That's why temperature should be high on your list of creature comforts. Insulate wherever possible then, if necessary, purchase a space heater and fan. Playtime's no time to save on energy—sexual or otherwise.

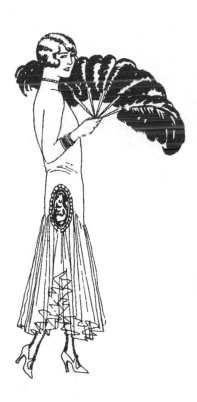

FRIGID FRANNIE'S FAN CLUB

"If I've said it once, I've said it a thousand times—getting custody of the thermostat was one of the best decrees in my divorce. Previously, with my "X" in charge, seasons never changed in our bedroom. I always froze my buns off and those icy temperatures did nothing to warm the cockles of my heart. I remember bathing nightly then donning flannel PJs, socks and a heavy robe. Bundled like a papoose, I couldn't turn myself on much less my husband. I always imagined lace negligees being gifts given at bridal showers. I would never dream of dressing that scantily and surviving the frigid air.

After our separation, I salvaged my frozen *ass-ets*, moved into a cozy home and controlled the thermostat. Now, I find it absolutely liberating to lounge nude on the bed. When hot weather arrives, I position a fan to blow over my bare bod. Legs open and knees bent, the air playfully osculates *fan-tastically* across my love areas. I'm perfectly content being a self-sexual single woman; however, if an appealing playmate pops up, my credo is simple: "Join my fan club or butt out buster."

Chair Leader

Women erotically aware make room for a chair. They know it's used for more than sitting or plunking clothes on. Space permitting, a chaise lounge is an alluring accessory, since you can position yourself in a variety of pleasurable ways. A Victorian rocker or wicker chair with plump cushions and matching ottoman keeps you sitting pretty. A thick, overstuffed armchair or recliner can elevate eroticism. Almost any chair could be useful for amour and more. What's this, you'd love adding a neat seat but, there's no room? Suspend your derrière in an artsy, woven swing. Requiring no floor space, it can be slipped off the hook when swinging sessions are put to sleep.

Beddy Buys

You can decorate a steamy sanctuary without making a big deal, but have a plan in mind. Pick a theme, borrowing ideas from magazines, furniture stores and model homes. Here are some imaginative ideas:

- Hang a self-stick wallpaper border around ceiling.
- Paint one wall a favorite color to add drama.

- Pile pillows adorned with flowers and ribbons. Hint: use space inside zippered pillows or shams to stash toys.
- Drape netting on wall behind bed, letting it stream seductively over and down sides of headboard.
- Gather lace or sheer fabric on a curtain rod then arrange artfully around window shades.
- Strategically place a full-length mirror where it can be viewed seductively. Mirrored strips can easily be hung with self-stick tape.
- Line drawers with decorative perfumed paper, set out potpourri, use scented ceramic lamp rings or aromatic essence. Change fragrance with sheets.

💜 Repaint old furniture and give it a face-lift by adding new handles, store clutter in decorative baskets, cover light switches with lace and pearls, accent room with a tri-fold dressing screen.

Use the following checklist to plan your playground:

SELECT A THEME FOR YOUR SCHEME

_____ Seductive _____ Romantic _____ Tranquil _____ Heavenly _____ Passionate

Wall color_____   Accent/Accessory Color _____

Think of five items that will make a difference (for example, a picture, aroma bottles, silk flowers, pillows, mirror, decorative fan, hanging plants, accent lighting, etc.)

1. _____
2. _____
3. _____
4. _____
5. _____

Personalize accessories with satin ribbons, faux jewels, ruffles, lace and permanent markers.

Don't Fall Asleep on the Job . . . Yawn

As a boring bedroom doesn't stimulate anything or any body, make your boudoir an invitation to seduction. These suggestions are aphrodisiacs that make a subtle but substantial difference between so-so or super self-pleasuring. Wake up Sleeping Beauty, it's time to stir up some bedroom bedlam. On your *Mark*, get *Seth* and go for it!

Privacy—Keep Out, Adult at Play

Caught with Your Pants Down (pant, pant)

Nothing's more inhibiting to unbridled sex than thinking someone will meander in and catch you bottoms up, bikini down. Haven't we all either walked in on someone or had them barge in on us while involved in something clandestine in nature. Even if the intruder excuses himself/herself immediately, the mood is muddled. Privacy is essential to effective eroticism.

Easier Said Than Done

If you share your humble abode, securing privacy may seem the impossible dream. Whether contending with children, guests or roommates, there are ways to insure uninterrupted encounters. A little advance preparation can protect sexy seclusion in the midst of mayhem. Since everyone deserves time, place and space to let their clothes and guard down, let's lock in a workable solution.

Don't Knock It

Time is a precious commodity we seldom spend on ourselves. You may give it away willingly or have it stolen by intruding phone calls and pint-sized distractions. It's your responsibility to recognize interruptions and decide how to handle them. Whether for emotional or sexual reasons, there's nothing wrong with establishing closed-door policies for set lengths of time. Even if not involved in something intimate, set a privacy program making others adjust to the idea. It's you who teach people to honor your privacy.

Solitary Confinement

Replying to a reader who wanted help on this subject, a well-known advice columnist replied, "If you want company, open the door; if you want privacy, close it. If you require security, lock it!"

"If you want company, open the door; if you want privacy, close it.

If you want security, lock it!"

VANITY FAIR

"Around my house it's easier asking for a hundred dollars than an hour's privacy. Locking my bedroom door is out of the question since it arouses more curiosity from my three kids than anything else. That's why I keep my joy toys hidden in a locked case among the toiletries in my bathroom vanity. It may seem strange, but self-pleasuring is my way of easing tension. When times get tough, this hassled mom heads for sanctuary in the bathroom. Sure, I'd rather be in bed, but the bathroom arouses less suspicion. My routine doesn't vary much—the exhaust fan, radio, then vibrator go on, in that order. I may shimmy on the vanity sink with legs up or slouch down on the rug. It doesn't much matter where I end up since I always finish relaxed, relieved and smiling."

For guaranteed moments alone, install a good door lock on a room of choice. For most this would be the bedroom; however, to keep her sanity, Isadora kept her vanity elsewhere.

Although I dislike wasting natural resources, another bathroom ploy used to discourage eavesdroppers is the sound of running water. A married woman I worked with also hid her habit behind the bathroom door. Sue-Ellen stashed her vibrator in the linen closet, and while her husband was in another room watching TV or "doing his own *thing,*" she'd turn on her blow dryer, then vibrator, and give herself a quickie. To this day her husband wonders why her hair is always damp when she emerges. Only her hairdresser knows for sure.

Now Hear This

How do you know when a little noise is too much? Check out the room acoustics before worrying how far itty-bitty sounds carry. If you enjoy using a vibrator (and who doesn't?) haven't you wondered if those outside the room can hear the hum? Sometimes we're overly self-conscious about being overheard and think every decibel is audible, regardless of how many barriers we put up. If you're afraid as I was that the walls have ears, take the following hearing test.

HEARING AID

"Being positively paranoid and sure my kids could detect a vibrator hum, I tested it while home alone. Setting the scenario, I turned on a vibe, left the room and shut the door before pressing an ear against it. Whew, I couldn't hear a thing. Undoubtedly, some machines are noisier than others, although they usually sound louder because you're on top of them. If yours is extra noisy, test with radio, cassette or TV turned on in the room."

Sound Barriers

Without calling in a team of engineers to sound-proof your home, take measures to eliminate noises. Tile and wood floors are beautiful, but resonant. Sound absorbers are carpeting, curtains and upholstered furniture. Heavy gauge wallpaper and mirrors also foster degrees of sound-proofing. Since most bedroom doors are hollow, covering one side with a full-length mirror provides a barrier of visible security. If the door doesn't fit flush to the floor, keep sounds in and prying eyes out by attaching self-stick weather stripping or rolled-up towel laid along the threshold.

For Your Ears Only

You can camouflage intimate activities with various sound screens. TV is distracting but it works. So will erotic videos with muted volume. I make certain to be silent during solo sex, saving my moans, groans and giggles for times with my partner. If you're a noisemaker, place a radio beside the door to cover sexy sounds. If, however, you're a screamer, nothing less than the Boston Pops Orchestra will drown out the noise.

BEAR-LY HEARD A THING

"I've lived with female roommates since college, and we'd never intrude on one another's space. My prime concern was that they'd overhear noises from my vibrator and/or significant other. My quest for privacy produced two tactics. The first is stashing a vibrator inside a teddy bear named "Love Stuff," designed with a zippered pouch to hold nighties . . . not nightly pleasures. With Love Stuff cuddling the vibe, bear-ly a sound can be heard.

When using a vibrating dildo, I'll lay over a pillow on my stomach. Not only is this my favorite position, but sandwiched between body and pillow, the toy can't be heard. Actually, the raunchiest racket comes from me. During orgasm, I tend to let out a series of squeaks and, every so often, I hit an out-of-tune high "C." Now that's what I call a problem! *OK, can you C?*"

Sign Language

In addition to that locked door, use humor to get your message across to house mates. Make *a-door-able* signs to hang on knobs that send clear signals to space invaders. Then tie one of these on for sighs:

Do Not Disturb (I'm Disturbed Already)

Frankly, my dear,
I vant to be alone!

Hear-Ye, Hear Me

The Princess is not receiving visitors at this time. Bother me and you'll be crowned!

Mirrors—Worth Looking Into

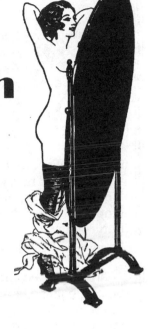

Let's Face It

Can you walk past a mirror or store window without sneaking a peek at your reflection? I can't. This is a vivid example of how concerned we are with appearance. Unlike us, small children openly delight in watching themselves. They have no qualms about smiling at their image and rejoicing in what they see . . . something everyone can learn from. We spend hours peering critically at our clothes, face and hair, but how often do we approve of it? Furthermore, do we take time to look lovingly at our bare bodies? There's much we can discover about ourselves in only one session in front of a mirror. Vanity? Narcissism? Nope! It's a healthy form of self-love and a super learning experience.

What You See Isn't Always What You've Got

Most men think nothing of letting it all hang out before a mirror, flexing a muscle here, and especially *there*. Women, however, feel less at ease viewing themselves in the buff. Is there a female on the face of the earth who hasn't felt anxious about her lover's reaction to seeing her naked? I'm betting we're not too different when it comes to critiquing our bodies. Perhaps you'll feel more at ease reading what I went through baring it all during intimacy.

REFLECTIONS

Looking back, I clearly remember having a ton of overly exaggerated hang-ups about my body. As a result, I became a mistress of disguise and carefully planned my wardrobe to accentuate the positives and eliminate the negatives. Dressed, I was confident and looked as if I had it all together. Ahhh, but during intimate interludes when my clothes came off, I was stripped of my confidence and panicked. Without taking quick action, I was sure he'd notice my imagined imperfections: thunder thighs, big butt, cellulite, and so on. Consequently, I'd pull out all sexual stoppers to turn him on. The rational was, if he stayed outrageously thrilled with my sexual expertise, he'd never spot my few flaws. Unfortunately, **my** sexual satisfaction got lost in the shuffle.

Ironically, no men seemed concerned if they had bulging bellies, balding heads, beefy thighs, too much here, not enough *there*. Not for one second did their physical short-comings affect their "coming." Giving so much of myself, my partner invariably returned for encores. Still, my self-confidence registered minus 10 on the Richter scale. Allowing my mind tp sabotage my body's responses, this sorry scenario played out for years. Except for private self-pleasuring, gratification was a gift I gave and never allowed myself to fully receive.

Dumping Dissatisfaction

It was during a solo encounter that I realized how low self-esteem undermined my intimacy and ability to climax with a partner. I knew these inhibitions would continue until I accepted what I couldn't change about my body and fixed what I could. With my usual enthusiasm, I threw mind, body and spirit into a crash course of self-improvement and sexual empowerment. Now began the adventure of working from the inside out—*feeling good* about my image, as well as *looking good*. I read stacks of self-help books and attended women's workshops. Exercise, nutritional savvy, mirror affirmations and a healthy awareness brought positive results. The naked truth is I pulled myself together and you can too!

Dare to Be Aware

How many of us can go to the mirror, look into our eyes and repeat that verse with meaningful self-love? Go ahead and try it, with one rule: no primping. _____

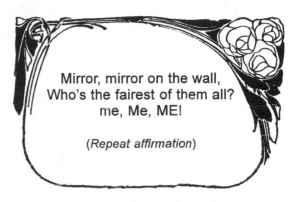

Mirror, mirror on the wall,
Who's the fairest of them all?
me, Me, ME!

(Repeat affirmation)

Okay, time's up! For most females, the ability to love and accept their body isn't easy. It's not selfish or egotistical, but makes good sense to regard ourselves as beautiful women, every bit as worthwhile as the men in our lives. Thoughts are tools of power, and anything you believe about yourself, **you** can make reality. Become your own best friend, instead of your worst enemy.

If you feel sensuous and *believe* you're a hot number, there's no doubt you'll portray that image. Sex therapist Judy Korenski aptly states, "Sex appeal comes from loving who you are." No matter how long you've been inside that body of yours, there are goodies galore to learn about having a fabulous, sexy self-image. Fall in love with yourself, then friends and lovers will beat a path to your door. Bernie Siegel, M.D., Wayne Dwyer Ph.D., Louise Hay and numerous renowned educators teach valuable self-love lessons. Include their books and tapes in your growing experience. Also, add fun to your repertoire with romantic antics.

Lookin' Good

Give a full-length mirror a try, only this time dare to bare. Observe yourself realistically from all angles while assessing your assets aloud. Listen attentively to your response. Look into those bedroom eyes and search out your true feelings. How critical are you of the reflected image? Do you see it as being too fat, thin, tall, short, unattractive, worthless, or unlovable? Are your breasts, hips, butt and stomach acceptable? Don't despair or tear out your hair. Instead, insert your hang-ups on the dotted lines:

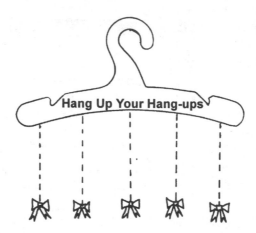

Hang Up Your Hang-ups

Great, now shove them in a closet, lock the door and throw away the key. There, you're positively perfect! It's time to realize self-acceptance is an attitude dictated by your brain. Stop making excuses, complaining and feeling sorry for yourself. Get to work on changing what you can. Use diet, exercise, make-over and, if necessary, cosmetic surgery. Accept and appreciate things you can't change. From this day on, every time you look at your captivating reflection give it **unconditional love**.

Journey from Berate to Liberate

> *"Nothing is good or bad, but thinking makes it so."*
> W. Shakespeare

When viewing your nakedness in the mirror and negativity pops up . . . don't get hysterical! Wink, smile, seductively shrug your shoulder and affirm: "Who can resist lovable me?" Stand tall, strut, slink, pose or stretch and belt out, "Baby, you got it." Blow extra kisses to scars, wrinkles, veins or other less-than-perfect areas. Accept them as trials and recorded history of where you've been. Use the mirror to watch yourself dance or prance till it feels good and looks inviting. Giggle, laugh, sing and rejoice at being the heavenly love goddess you are. Remember, keep repeating positive affirmations until they become a part of you.

The Bod Squad

For me, gaining bodily self-confidence was an awakening. It relieved anxieties in and out of the bedroom. Want to see magic happen for you? Do daily affirmations. Start with, "Good morning, gorgeous" in the bathroom mirror. Doesn't it sound much better than, "Good grief, it's morning and my face needs a miracle"? Place reminders on self-stick notes and place on mirrors, the fridge, in your car and at work as prompts to continue positive self-talk. Repeat until believable.

Whenever a negative thought pops up, imagine a huge rubber stamp with the word **cancel** over it, eradicating its *de-meaning*. Make up your own uplifting, complimentary phrases or use some of these tried and true ones:

AFFIRMING THE POSITIVE MIRROR EXERCISES

Do several times daily to improve your life, looks and outlook.

I love and approve of myself. My experiences are joyous and rewarding. C.R.

I open up and express the beauty and love of life. S.V.

I'm fully deserving of love and respect I freely give others. J.M.

I attract sharing, caring people in my life now. P.F.

I am perfectly happy to be me. I am good enough just as I am. I love and approve of myself. I am joy expressing and receiving. Louise Hay

My life is joyful, exciting and sexually satisfying. G.L.

My body, mind, spirit and sexuality are in perfect harmony and ready to share with a special someone. R.M.

I love and accept my sensuous body exactly as it is. A.T.

Gaining self-confidence may take weeks, months or longer. Enjoy the journey of self-discovery until you reap the joy. For additional help, get motivational tapes, books, how-to videos, sign up for dance, exercise or awareness classes. Make a plan and do it now!

Dis-robe-ics

A dancer's seductive movements have always served a particular purpose. Salome stunningly mesmerized emperor Herod with her gyrations and John the Baptist lost his head over it . . . . ouch! These days, free-style fancy footwork has been known to capture a heart and a lot more. Performed privately in front of a mirror, it can tone your body, get circulation perking and up confidence in both the dance and romance department.

Enjoy starring in your personal foxy lady productions with ploys, pantomime and panache. Without further fanfare, enter the prop room, set the scene, get ready, step, GO . . . Aaannnd ACTION!!!

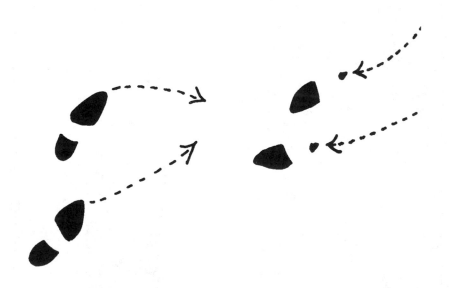

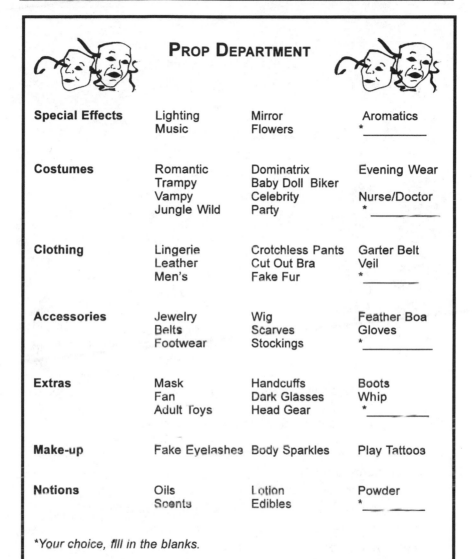

PROP DEPARTMENT

Special Effects	Lighting Music	Mirror Flowers	Aromatics *_____
Costumes	Romantic Trampy Vampy Jungle Wild	Dominatrix Baby Doll Biker Celebrity Party	Evening Wear Nurse/Doctor *_____
Clothing	Lingerie Leather Men's	Crotchless Pants Cut Out Bra Fake Fur	Garter Belt Veil *_____
Accessories	Jewelry Belts Footwear	Wig Scarves Stockings	Feather Boa Gloves *_____
Extras	Mask Fan Adult Toys	Handcuffs Dark Glasses Head Gear	Boots Whip *_____
Make-up	Fake Eyelashes	Body Sparkles	Play Tattoos
Notions	Oils Scents	Lotion Edibles	Powder *_____

*Your choice, fill in the blanks.

Gather props and prepare to star in your own self-pleasure production. C'mon "daaahling," get wild and crazy. Dim the lights, and on with the show.

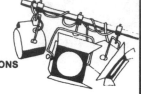
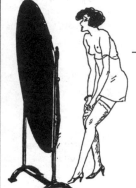

FOXY SELF-PLEASURE PRODUCTIONS

PRESENTS

SHOW-OFF TIME
Starring

_____

(your name)

in

Sunset Strip

> ### CUE
> **Smile and make eye contact with your stunning reflection.**

Stand in front of a full-length mirror while dressed and start doing a sensual strip. Open one button at a time or s-l-o-w-l-y unzip. Shimmy out of your top and fling it off with a flourish.

★ With hands on hips and shoulders erect, arch back, thrust chest out and shake about.
★ Slither out of slacks or skirt.
★ Undulate hips, swiveling side to side, back and forth.
★ Prance and parade seductively in your undies.
★ Point toes, pirouette and spin around admiring your feminine form from all angles.
★ With bra on, stroke breasts; stage a sneak preview, sliding a finger or two inside your panties.
★ À la Gypsy Rose Lee and take it off, take it all off!
★ Become a loose goose. Bend, stretch, roll shoulders, spread legs. Outrageously show your star quality.

Tell the mirror, "You ain't seen nothing yet, the best is yet to come" . . . and **it is**!

FOXY SELF-PLEASURE PRODUCTIONS

PRESENTS

SHOW-OFF TIME
Starring

_____

(your name)

in

Flesh Dance

> ### CUE
> **Flirt with friend in the mirror. Raise an eyebrow seductively and wink.**

Dress up, put a silk rose in your hair, get dancing heels on and do a floozy flamenco. Ta da! How about a few high kicks à la Rockets? Don't simply go through the motions—energize while lifting your thighs. Now vary the repertoire:

★ Pile on jangly chains, then with a wig and wiggle shake it up baby, twist 'n shout.

★ Raise arms overhead, palms together, frame face and belly dance.

★ Shimmy, gyrate and roll hips, mimicking moves of wild lovemaking.

★ Up the beat and give it your best Saturday night fervor. Exaggerate movements, be suggestive and really turn yourself on.

★ Work at achieving a fun, funky and frankly sexy style.

★ Let hair and inhibitions down.

You have two left feet? No excuse. Adult ed offers classes in everything from cha-cha to country. For those who'd rather hoofer at home, rent how-to videos or tune in VH1. See how dancing enhances and improves your image and intimacy. Want personalized instructions? Alan, Alfonse or Arthur Murray will happily teach dancing with a flurry.

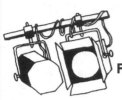

Foxy Self-Pleasure Productions
PRESENTS
Show-Off Time
Starring

(your name)
in
Dressed to Thrill

> ### Cue
> **Pucker up, lick your lips and blow kisses to that stunning reflection.**

Become your own wardrobe mistress using a variety of clothes encounters of a sexual kind:

Act One: Sex Kitten

Use a wig or tease hair wildly. Don leopard print or other jungle attire and prowl around like a ferocious jungle cat. Get on all fours, arch your back, stretch and do a slinky cat-walk. Bend head then toss it back from side to side, flinging hair over shoulders. Growl or purr loudly . . . grrrreat!

Act Two: Teddy Bare

For another "seen," wear a titillating teddy. Glide around like a vamp oozing seduction. Luxuriate in sensations the fabric elicits hugging your body. While gazing at your every move, rub, pinch, tweak and stroke yourself absolutely everywhere. Point your finger at the mirror making a come hither gesture asking, "Mmm, who can resist me?"

Act Three: Gushing Geisha

Pin up hair, paint and powder your face, then slip into an Oriental kimono. Let it fall open as you flit about like Madam Flutterby.

Dance demurely about using a fan and your fanny, too. Develop a style that will bring him to his knees. End by bowing like a geisha. Sayonara.

Act Four: Material Girl

Take a long scarf and dramatically drape it around your body. Twirl about admiring yourself while savoring the feel of the fabric caressing your skin. Romp around as if planning to seduce your favorite celeb. Remove the veil and extend it between outstretched arms. Focus on your image while rubbing the sheer fabric briskly across breasts then buttocks. Finally, place it between your legs, grab each end and seductively slide it back and forth across your genitals creating friction and hot times.

Act Five: Lace to Lust

Make the most of a peek-a-boo bra, crotchless panties and string of pearls. Pull on a pair of thigh-high hose or that classic put-on, a garter belt and mesh stockings. Slip into trampy spiked heels, strut your stuff and whirl pearls provocatively around. What a babe! Thinking whip cream thoughts, roll tongue around your dewy lips, then throw yourself a luscious kiss . . . smack!

Exit Laughing

Now that you've starred in the foxy "for-play" production, dim the lights and, if so inclined, recline on the casting couch with or without your favorite director for the grand finale. What a talent. No doubt you'll get first billing.

Here's looking at you kid and you know what? You're lookin' good!

Skin Slicks—
Lotions, Potions
and Notions

Things You Auto Know

Honk if you're horny—Beep, Beep! This chapter doesn't pertain to tuning up your car, it's about charging your chassis. Not a crash course in Driver's Ed., rather another vehicle to boost auto-eroticism, with or without assistance from *Mr. "Goodwrench."*

Shift into High Gear . . . Dear

Lotions and oils have been part of sensuous rituals since ancient times. Slick chicks knew then what you're about to learn: Lubricants applied to your own or a fellow passenger's skin help us discover where our bodies are most receptive to touch. Smoothing on key components keeps motors purring and adds fuel to middle-of-the road masturbation.

Skin-y Dipping

Which lubes to use and where to apply them is strictly personal preference. Some find lotions too gooey to mess with. Others feel it revs up their engine, eliciting high-speed thrills while touring hot spots. Either one keeps skin satiny soft while preventing wear and tear on movin' 'n groovin' parts . . . you're **not** just lying there, are you?

Smart Women, Fuelish Choices

Here's how skin slicks jump start sexuality, putting you in the driver's seat.

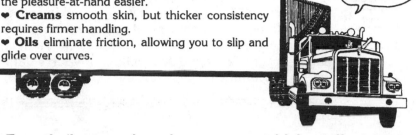

❤ **Lotions** amplify touch which makes focusing on the pleasure-at-hand easier.
❤ **Creams** smooth skin, but thicker consistency requires firmer handling.
❤ **Oils** eliminate friction, allowing you to slip and glide over curves.

"Jeff E. Lube to the rescue"

Even if oil prices skyrocket, commercial lubes offer inexpensive, innovative ways to pamper self or shared joyrides. Premium grades from sex shops have higher prices, not necessarily higher octane. If skin is ultrasensitive, bypass products containing perfumes or irritating chemicals. Test drive them all, opting for natural ingredients for zing, not sting.

X -Rated Additives

"Drivers" desiring a grand prix thrill should check out the following high performance lubes. Reading the hype for sex shop slicks will give you almost as large a charge as using them . . . .

HOT STUFF

Do yourself a favor by trying hot 'n tasty *motion lotions* (which are actually oils). They're the most popular adult skin slicks since they warm to the touch and/or breath. Because these liquids are thick and not quickly absorbed, skin stays sticky until it's licked or washed off. On unaccompanied seXcursions, use "Hot Stuff" rubbed around navel, nipples and other points of interest. During shared encounters, use fingers or massager to blaze a trail over raunchy routes. You and a fellow commuter can light one another's fire by blowing on, then licking applied area, using caution or your/his engine may prematurely overheat! Hot stuff is available in piña colada, chocolate, cinnamon, and everyone's favorite, wild cherry. Raise your temperature with **Heat Wave**, **Emotion Lotion** and **Act of Love**.

SWELL JELLS

It looks like jelly and spreads like jam . . . what a heck-of-a-gel for a belle. Jells are strictly for fun but become sticky if allowed to dry, so flick or lick'em off quickly. Play artist with pasty, tasty water-based gel body paints. With a partner joining this jam session, fingerpaint or brush on terms of endearments or directions to follow. ☞ ∂∂ "Erase" mistakes with a little tongue action. Test drive **Joy Jell**, **Strawberry Jam** and **Fruit Yummies**.

STRIKING OIL

Real women pump oil. They give incredible *s'mileage* with merely a few drops, making shifting into high gear smoother. On pleasure trips, Slicks are guaranteed to go the distance. For a rousing massage, glide them on with a wand or multi-attachment vibrator using the *facial tip* attachment. Some premium blended products contain flavors and scents that produce warm, tingling sensations. Be aware, oils are crude as well as lewd, meaning they disintegrate latex condoms, diaphragms and toys. Although not recommended for internal use, he'll enjoy them massaged on his "dipstick." Oils to gush over are **Charlie Sunshine**, **Kama Sutra Oil of Love** and **Natural Vitamin E Massage Oil** (my personal favorite). Easily concoct your own healthy version (minus the warming additive) varying the following recipe.

OIL OF OHHH LAY

Edible Spreadable Potion
1/2 cup sesame, peanut or canola oil
12 drops of natural oil-based food extract (flavor of choice)
Place in flip-top bottle shaking well to blend.

Non-Edible Aromatherapy Massage Formula
1/2 cup sesame, peanut or canola oil
4 drops each of essential oils—Ginger, jasmine and coriander
Place in flip-top bottle shaking to blend.

Lubes for Internal Combustion

Ever feel so dry you could cry? You've got plenty of company. Most females, regardless of age, experience vaginal dryness some time. This may be due to: monthly cycle, menopause, medication, tampons, stress and so forth. Certainly it doesn't mean you're not turned on or your partner is doing something wrong. More women than you might realize rely on lubes. When it comes time to fill-er-up, a little dab should do ya!

In-Slide Information

Besides being irritating, perfumes, alcohol, petroleum, or baby oil interfere with the vagina's natural protection against infection. Other than saliva, water-soluble gels are safe, satisfying and smooth ways to enhance penetration without dam-aging condoms. Be playful when dabbing lubes on your joy toy . . . or boy toy; it'll drive him nuts. Instead of fretting about a lack of moisture, use these safe lubes and stay wet and wild:

♥ **Replens:** Single use, pre-filled applicator. Replenishes vaginal moisture and lasts for days. Applied in advance, it allows sexual spontaneity.

♥ **Lubrin:** Long-lasting lubricating insert.

♥ **K-Y Jelly, Astro Glide, Wet, Foreplay:** Effective vaginal moisturizers. Some contain Nonoxynol-9 to protect against germs as well as sperms.

Take a Powder

Here's dusting you'll adore doing—sprinkling skin with powder. It adds silkiness, sans moisture, and is a delightfully dry way of minimizing friction on body parts. Provocatively fluff or feather on. Cotton candy flavored **Tickled Pink** and erotically spicy **Kuma Sutra** are both packaged with feathered applicators at adult stores.

Most commercial powders contain talc, which is unhealthy to inhale. Better yet are store-bought products containing cornstarch. Pardon my dust but, being an erotic yet slightly neurotic health nut, I mix my own pampering powder.

PUFF-STUFF

1 cup cornstarch
Few drops of vanilla, cherry, mint or other natural food flavoring
1 wide-mouth, spout top plastic container (like those used to dispense mustard or ketchup)

Put cornstarch in container. Add flavoring. Cap tightly, then shake it up baby. *Voila*—a healthy substitute for a pittance of the price of sex shop sprinkle stuff.

Recipe for Kicking Up a Little Dust

Dip a stiff feather into powder and flick around underarms, nipples, clitoris or inner thighs. Or powder hot spots using a soft artist or cosmetic brush. (I've even used a new feather duster . . . it's the only dusting I enjoy.)

Crème de la Cream

So you don't get creamed checking out boxcars of body lotions, travel the *au-naturel* route. These wholesome products contain dizzying arrays of herbs, fruits, flower essences and earthy ingredients plus aromatic fragrances that fill up the senses. They're a loving way to lavish our largest erogenous zone—the skin.

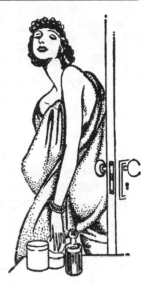

Heightened environmental awareness plus taking responsibility for our personal health are making an impact. As a result, more companies offer back-to-nature products which sensitively shun animal testing and save rain forests. Beyond the moral majority of reasons to use them, botanical formulas are good for you and our planet, too!

Bumper to Bumper Detailing

Since creams and lotions absorb quicker than oils, they may not be the slicks of choice for a lengthy session of sexual adventuring. Ahhh, but how about using them as an affirmation of loving the skin you're in and a prelude of what's to come? Indulge and lift your libido by slathering on rich moisturizers after a relaxing bath or shower. Take time to lovingly caress every curve and crevice. You'll hardly make it to the bedroom!

Add Fuel to Your Fetish

Adult-R-rated stores tempt us with potions to rub on every thigh-way and sigh-way. Two brands are: **Creme de Massage** in tasty almond, passion fruit or cherry jubilee, and almond-scented **Kuma Sutra Massage Cream**. Both formulas rub you the right way during play or before it's time to *re-tire* . . .

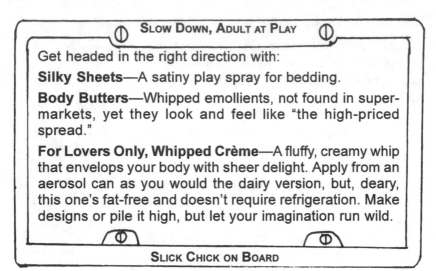

SLOW DOWN, ADULT AT PLAY

Get headed in the right direction with:

Silky Sheets—A satiny play spray for bedding.

Body Butters—Whipped emollients, not found in super-markets, yet they look and feel like "the high-priced spread."

For Lovers Only, Whipped Crème—A fluffy, creamy whip that envelops your body with sheer delight. Apply from an aerosol can as you would the dairy version, but, deary, this one's fat-free and doesn't require refrigeration. Make designs or pile it high, but let your imagination run wild.

SLICK CHICK ON BOARD

Some for the Road

You're at the wheel when it comes to pumping up sexual satisfaction. Skin slicks are another vehicle that can spark up a deflated routine. One thing's for sure—lubes are the ticket for a smoother ride. Buff over your chassis, his rear bumper, instrument panel, or . . . ah um, spare tire. You'll speedily discover "auto-erotic" doesn't mean loving your car.

Vrooommmm!

13 ♥ Perfume— Become a Scent-uous Woman

Friends, Romans, Countrywomen . . . Lend Me Your Airs

Since ancient times, fragrance has played a primary role in the enhancement of emotion. Thousands of years ago, Romans, Greeks and Egyptians used plant extracts, spices and perfumed ointments for therapy, attracting and making love. The Egyptians believed aromatic oils were created by the gods and placed scent in high esteem. It was, however, hedonistic Romans who deserve credit for enhancing the ability of fragrance to delight the senses and sensuality. Before Rome burned, Nero did more than just fiddle. He ingeniously installed pipes to continually spray perfume throughout his royal palace when frolicking with his femme fatales.

Back to the Future

Today, growing numbers of people are going back in time with natural and manufactured scents. They're discovering the many earthy delights of interweaving fragrance into their daily experiences . . . in and out of the boudoir. How are aromatics able to move and motivate? What makes them touch our heart and play games with our psyche? Read on.

The Nose Knows

Here's how sense of smell stirs up desire, awakens the body's capabilities and greatly affects mind, spirit and sensuality. When odor molecules enter our nose they float merrily along, triggering nerve receptors connected to the brain. These mini molecules move like busy bees to meet with nerve reactors, instantly causing hormones to respond. The effect of scent on psyche is potent, immediate and very real indeed.

Pour on Amour

Toujours l'amour, tonight for sure? Simply rub scent here, dab there or spray the air. Undoubtedly you'll be kicking up your heels in no time. Most of us don't consciously realize how important pleasant aromas are to libido unless we lose our sense of smell. People with odor disorders sometimes develop ardor dysfunction and may lose interest in sex. Aromas absolutely affect frame of mind and body much like soft lighting, beautiful music and so forth.

Since sense of smell heightens when becoming aroused, fragrance on or around our body gets us in an amorous mood. We inhale over 24,000 times each day, so why not incorporate light scent with heavy breathing? Don't save fragrance only for those times with a partner. If it makes you feel special with another, it'll have the same effect solo. A rose is more than merely a rose and can help you rise to the occasion of *scent-sational* sex for one.

Take a Scent-a-mental Journey

Welcome to the wonderful world of aroma therapy. Learn how enchantingly essential oils and specific scents from flowers, herbs and plants yield fragrance to help turn you into a *scent-ual* siren. Presented with playfulness, pick a posy or heavenly herb that's superb for spicing up sexiness.

Become an adventurous spirit, and fling the gates open to an enchanting garden of aromatic delights. Without tiptoeing through the tulips it's possible to: fantasize frolicking in a field of frankincense, jump joyously among jasmine, or do your thing on a bed

Chamomile: Serene
Clary Sage: Relieves stress
Eucalyptus: Balances energy
Frankincense: Stimulating
Geranium: Uplifting
Jasmine: Aphrodisiac
Lemon: Uplifting
Myrrh: Woody
Neroli: Soothing
Patchouli: Musty
Peppermint: Refreshing
Sandalwood: Elevates moods
Thyme: Uplifting
Vetiver: Earthy
Ylang Ylang: Aphrodisiac

of roses. Follow your nose as you enter a haven of *au naturel* elation for a healthy high that can breathe new life into sexual solitaire.

Tea-rific Tea-sers and Pleasers

Another serene way to take a breather from daily drudgery and set a loving mood is with fragrant, flavorful herb tea. Pour it steaming into a beautiful teacup and inhale the heady aroma as you sip, or serve it iced in a long-stemmed crystal goblet. Ingesting any of the following teas could perk up sexual desires:

Damiana (my all time favorite), Fenugreek, Ginseng, Licorice, Safflower, Sarsaparilla and Slippery Elm.

Available in health stores is a special blend of traditional herbs that tone hormones and enhance sexual vitality. It's appropriately named *Sensuali-tea, "A Potent Brew for Lovers."* It contains: rose petals, muira puama, cinnamon, spearmint, licorice, ho shou wu, damiana, hawthorn, sarsaparilla, coriander, nutmeg and cloves. Hint: avoid sage, skullcap, willow and hops as they are sexual depressants.

Scents-able Fun-for-One Solutions

Capture the rapture of erotic pleasures with essential oils. Use singly or blend into lotions, massage oils, candles, air fresheners, sachets, and potpourri. Merely a drop or two is long-lasting and will uplift you emotionally, spiritually and sexually. Use only one perfume at a time. The good news is it learns fast. Read how a variety of pleasure-seeking females *auto-magically* enhance their *auto-erotic* endeavors.

La Fleurs d'Amour

You're invited to a garden party of sorts. Meet a bunch of American beauties who will teach you about the sweet smell of *sex-cess.* Read how they cultivate their field of dreams and play it with flowers, using fragrance to make their solo and shared sex lives nothing short of *scent-sational.* No clinging vines or wallflowers here but perhaps you'll meet a few wildflowers. Only their names have been changed to add whimsy. Turn over a new leaf and become one of the flowers that bloom on the (bed)springs, and smile, if your "t'horny." Hoe, hoe, hoe!

"Call me silly Lily, but here's a dilly of a way I satiate my sexual appetite. I love languishing on a bed enveloped with floral printed sheets and sprayed lightly with scent. For good measure, I'll tuck sachets with concentrated aroma inside pillow shams piled high against the headboard. This entices me and my steady beddy-buddy when he romping on my garden of earthy delights. Additionally, I apply flavorful food extracts, such as crème de menthe and, of course, chocolate, on my shoulders, wrists and fingers, then slowly lick it off. Since I'm kind of buxom, I dab a drop on my boobs and . . . well, use your imagination. With a playmate over, flavorful extracts get us going lickety-split."

"I'm in love with scent so I saturate cotton balls and put them in closets, drawers, lingerie and bedding. Sometimes, I forgo fragrance until I get a whiff of something wonderful, then I start those cotton balls rolling all over again. I've discovered, after constant use, that my nose gets immune to a scent, so I'm fickle with fragrance . . . pretty much like I am with my adult boys and toys."

"I'm what you might call a shy violet, preferring to spend quality time with myself. To add ambiance, I burn incense, simmer potpourri or light perfumed candles, while meditating, masturbating or making love. Another way I add magic to my cozy apartment is with an aroma lamp. I simply add drops of essential oil to water in the glass container and light a candle below it. As I lay on my plush furry rug, the lamp throws off alluring combinations of shape, color, light and fragrance melting my shyness away."

**OSE** "Flowers are my passion and, true to my name, I lavish my body and home with . . . you guessed it . . . roses! My favorite fragrance is essence of tea rose. I have a special collection of clay jewelry that holds essential oils. Wearing these necklaces and pins, the scent follows wherever I stray or play. Another perfume ploy I enjoy is placing fragrance directly on my bedroom light bulb. When the light's on, the bulb's heat releases alluring aroma. After it's lights out, the scent continues to waft seductively about Rose's nose and toes."

**RIS** "I truly enjoy essential oils. For daytime it's apple, lemon and gardenia; for playtime, frankincense, sandalwood and ylang ylang. Blending 3 parts vegetable oil with 1 part herbal essence and creates erotic euphoria. I'll lovingly dab it on pulse points and hot spots. If I don't have someone to do it for me, I'll teasingly and tenderly anoint myself with fragrant massage oil from head to toe and everywhere in between."

**AISY** "I never worry if 'he loves me or loves me not' and I don't wait to get beautiful bouquets thrown my way. Since flowers are my *second* favorite passion, I have a jungle of plants around my apartment, especially the boudoir. Because fresh buds aren't as long lasting, I keep a beautiful bunch of silk posies in a crystal vase next to my bed and spray them with essential oil. I also scent feathers, fluff and all the rest of my feminine finery—makes me feel special even when I don't have someone to tell me so . . . and I am, so there!"

OLLY "Whether I'm entertaining a friend or enjoying my own company, I get into fragrance. Usually I'll opt for men's colognes instead of women's, finding them less frilly, more unique. Their musky, woodsy aroma smells sexy on me. Men seem to relate to the trail I leave behind and beat a path to my door."

 **I**vy "I work and play hard—that's why I plan one night a week just for *moi*. Lacing a warm bath with scented oil, I'll bathe by glowing fragrant votives. Leaning back against a waterproof pillow, I'll fill up my senses, basking and breathing in the incredibly intoxicating aroma. I particularly savor the unique vibration each fragrance creates throughout my being. After 20 minutes, I emerge a new woman ready for *l'amour* and more."

Your Personal Purr-fume

On your journey to becoming a *self-scentuous* new you, take time to smell the roses. Wild, cultured or "hy-bred" flowers and females share a special beauty and individuality. The ones who refuse to bloom and grow go unnoticed. Life and love give back what you cultivate. You can surround yourself with all forms of beauty as you romp in a garden of self and shared seductions, or simply settle for something less. The choice is yours.

Water Play— May the Faucet Be with You

A Whale of a Tale

"It started so innocently. I stepped into the shower and sighed as warm water spilled sensually over my body. Droplets bounced off my breasts and rivulets cascaded onto my glistening pubic hair. Rinsing away the fatigue of the day felt fabulous as a surge of new energy enveloped mind and body.

Turning toward the sharp needles of spray made my nipples spring to attention. I lathered my now swollen breasts then began soaping my thighs. The steam seductively surrounded me and a I started throbbing deep within. My hands developed a mind of their own; one fondled a breast, the other commenced a frothy foray to my thirsty labial lips. I spread my legs and let water pulse against my throbbing clitoris before slipping a finger into the dewy depths. I was drenched with desire. Sooo good . . . no stopping now.

Needing something more, I grabbed the shower massager and directed the jet stream around both breasts. My skin prickled under the pressure and I winced at the stinging sensation. Determined to quench the yearnings, I straddled the massager, crushing my pubes against the outpouring flow. Moving up and down the pulsating "phallus," I moaned, drifting on a sea of ecstasy. Rising waves of rapture continued engulfing me. I sank to my knees as every nerve quivered under the tension. Suddenly the dam burst as undercurrents of my first "off-shore" orgasm swept me away . When the wave subsided I vowed never to wait so long before testing the waters again."

Think that story was about me? You're all wet! It's just one of many tales of aquatic adventuring I've been privy to. You too can write your own wet and wild script. Climb aboard matie—this love boat's headed for pleasure island with you at the helm.

Creating a Sensual Spa

Hardly anyone has a "House Beautiful" bathroom. Most of us make do with small stalls and tiny tubs which we can't even call our own. Don't, however, let this dampen your seaworthy spirit. With a sprinkling of imagination, transform your bathroom into a sensual spa of sorts. To make it a dreamy, steamy sanctuary, it's not necessary to have a whirlpool, pool man or pool all your resources.

It's All in Your Head

Before spreading your water wings, outfit the "head" (a nautical term for bathroom) with some affordable accessories:

- Install dimmer switches on bathroom lights, or use a night light and replace standard bulbs with pink ones—so soothing, sexy and flattering to every body.

- Place potted or hanging plants around the room, or decorate with live, silk or dried flowers.

- Assemble soaps, steamy reads, waterproof toys and joys. Place sensuous spa stuff in a decorative covered wicker basket that can be left out if you have a private bathroom. If it's a problem, stow gear in a pocketed hanging organizer.

- Put pictures on the walls that look lovely and make you feel feminine.

- Hang up your hang-ups along with sensuous, lacy lingerie or silky robe. Display your feminine finery on a satin hanger as a reminder that you're truly see-worthy serene.

- Use mirrors to make the bathroom look larger and reflect a sensual you.

- Fill Lucite containers with aromatic bath salts or potpourri.

- Hang up decorative, sumptuous towels to snuggle into after water play.

- A battery-powered, water safe shower radio sets a noteworthy mood.
- Now that everything's ship-shape, use your *a-door-able* "Out to Launch" sign to assure privacy, then dive in.

OUT TO LAUNCH

DO NOT DISTURB!

> **SOUND ADVICE**
> Keep electric appliances away from the H_2O.

I Love the Soaps

No, not "The Guiding Light" or "One Life to Live"—the kind of soaps I tune into are the natural, aromatic varieties. For good, clean, non-irritating fun, avoid using products with harsh chemicals, perfumes or artificial color. Instead, float your boat on down to a health store, specialized body or bath boutique. One popular organic product is called *Dr. Bronner's Wintergreen Castille*. Great while bathing, and especially exciting in the shower if slathered all over, dabbing extra on your clitoris and vaginal opening. Tingles last until you make it to the bedroom. Nurture your body with Aloe Vera, papaya, honey and other *au naturel* niceties. Opt for no-frill thrills and pamper your skin for pennies using oils such as olive or sesame. A few drops of almond or vanilla food extract adds fragrance.

Other Head-y Delights

Good old reliable *Herb* makes a perfect bathing companion. But if *he* isn't available try a variety of the following user friendly botanicals:

- **Aphrodisiacs**—ginger, mint and several other herbs.
- **Refreshing**—pine and mineral salts.
- **Skin softeners**—lavender, rosemary, thyme and oatmeal.
- **Relaxing and healing**—sprigs of chamomile and dried orange flowers.
- **Euphoric baths**—natural flower oils and bath salts.

The bliss list is endless, so experiment.

> ### PIPELINE POINTER
>
> Unless you have a plumber for a playmate, don't rock the boat by putting herbs, spices or potpourri directly into water as they'll clog the drain. To release fragrance, wrap them in cheesecloth or piece of hosiery. Tie securely and float, or hang in the path of running water.

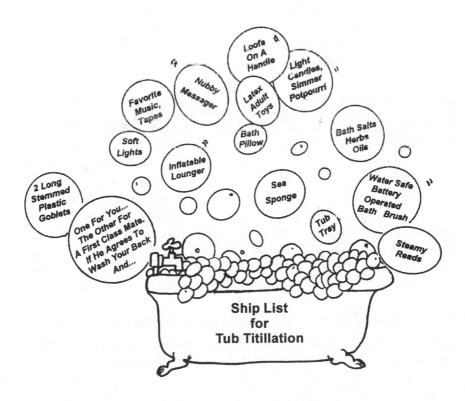

Ship List
for
Tub Titillation

Naughty-cal 'n Nice

Adult stores and specialty mail order companies offer a flotilla of down-under products. Fishing for a hot catch? Hook onto the following:

- **Slippery stuff**—specially formulated lotion that duplicates natural secretions and maintains its consistency in water.
- **Phallic-shaped glycerin**—not Moby but "Big Dick," a decadent hunk of soap that's swell to rub on in all directions; however, **never insert this or any soap.**
- **Finger ticklers**—hollow latex loaded with nibs and nubs to slip on a finger for breast stroking or intimate dipping.
- **Rubber dildos**—dive in and snag one of the many varieties of "pretend penises." Water-proof, battery-operated models abound in all sizes.

> ### TEPID TIP
> Invest in a few props and quit floundering around. Then playfully hike up your mainsail, with or without a main man.

Be a Jet Setter

Eliciting *wave reviews* are whirlpools and other bubbly baths. The powerful jets are extraordinary for relaxing some muscles, revving up others. Jacuzzi-style whirlpools and hot tubs are found in many homes, or with disposable income, portable units are up for grabs at moderate prices. They magically transform any tub into a cauldron of effervescent erotica. Straddle the jet stream, open wide and let the water pulsate around your clitoris. The feeling is much like a frenzy of fingers, tap, tap, tapping away. Actually, whole books could be written about hot times in hot tubs. Tempted? *Dew* drop in and come to your own conclusions.

Welcome Aboard the Fun Ship "X-ta Sea"

Many a *sailorette* finds a slippery, sexy water massage can be a *reel* lifesaver when stressed out. Once submerged, cast off inhibitions and refrain from thoughts of kids, chores or career. Instead, allow your mind to drift to fantasy land. Here's how to get underway:

- Lean back, close eyes and gently rub, stroke or pat face, neck and shoulders using hand or waterproof massager.

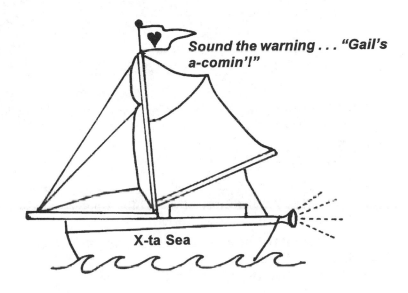

Sound the warning . . . "Gail's a-comin'!"

X-ta Sea

- Caress breasts and massage nipples, tweaking the sensitive peaks.
- Trace circles over belly before charting a course to your feet.
- Now lift and rub arch, instep and toes. Press and slide fingertips up calves of legs paying particular attention to backs of knees.
- Steer full steam ahead to insides of your opened thighs and apply kneading movements along with firm pressure.
- Concentrate on the tranquil feelings before sailing toward more provocative ports of entry.

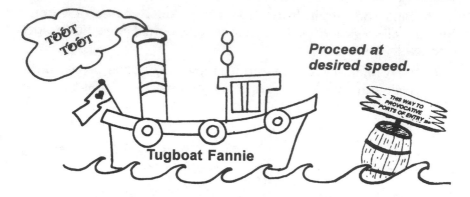

TOOT TOOT

Proceed at desired speed.

THIS WAY TO PROVOCATIVE PORTS OF ENTRY

Tugboat Fannie

♦ Grasp a handful of wet pubic hair and gently pull so it tugs at your clitoris.

♦ Slip a finger or waterproof toy into your moist love tunnel and drop anchor a while . . . .

♦ Plant your feet on either side of the faucet. Use legs to raise and lower yourself into bath water while undulating in currents. Prepare to come about!

Congratulations! You've navigated masterfully throughout the "hands-on" water course! Hope you've had oceans of fun. If not, don't throw in the towel—*sea* ya in the shower.

The Happy Hook-up

More water babes are indulging in wet play, with and without a salty *sea-man,* thanks in part to shower massagers. These hand-held devices replace standard shower heads. For erotic effects, select slow, fast or pulsating spray, and do more than wash troubles away:

♦ For starters, get your pulse churning by directing spray on breasts, buttocks and inner thighs.

♦ Squat down, spread knees apart and aim that heady flow directly on your clitoris.

♦ Open labia lips and seductively move the pulsating aquatic action up, down and all around.

♦ Use steady genital spraying along with manual manipulation. Batten the hatches; this may lead to a wet 'n wild orgasm.

Ladies Be Seated

Standing during water play is about as sexy as treading water and could be the reason many don't try shower sex. Thanks to vinyl coated shower seats, the standing-room-only problem's been solved. The seat is convenient for taking care of bothersome chores such as shaving sea legs, if for nothing else. When getting down to shower fun, it's the best seat in the house . . . at least for one mermaid named Lily . . .

Fantasy at Lily's Pond

"Guess I'm just a dreamer," Lily from Lauderdale relates. "I love fantasizing in the shower. In preparation, I'll pick up my rubber *duckie*, flick on a dim light, then enter the enclosure. After adjusting the water, I position myself on the seat: feet up on edges, legs parted. It always feels sensual to lean back, close my eyes and relax while the water flows over me. As the spray streams on to my bosom, belly and genital area, I vividly enact a fantasy. One of my favorite steamy stories is about being outdoors, nude, on a park bench with men all around watching me. My hands busily probe and stimulate my body as I imagine huge erections bulging inside their pants.

Pulling back the fleshy folds around my clitoris allows water to trickle, tickle and excite my hot bed of erupting erotica. The flow beats against my skin like torrents of rain. One hand massages my genitals, the other caresses my large breasts. I'll lift a bosom to my tongue and encircle the nipple; it's delightfully taut and tastes salty, but delicious. Soon both hands are busily squeezing and probing, attempting to satisfy my wild yearnings. I visualize the men's eyes transfixed on me, while their hands reach to touch and satisfy the large, throbbing desire between their legs.

As excitement mounts, in a frenzy of sexual passion, I grab the dildo and passionately insert it as I would a lover's penis. One hand latches onto my dripping mound, the other repeatedly propels the "pretend penis." My pelvis rhythmically gyrates until I can't hold back. Finally, I burst in *lightning* climaxes, beneath the downpour of my stormy shower.

Maiden Voyage

Now, fair maiden, are you ready to let the good times flow? Once you surrender and enjoy the sybaritic feeling water elicits, I'm sure you'll have a whale of a tale of your own to tell. Whether you dip, dunk, percolate or plunge, a vast treasure of buried pleasure awaits your arrival somewhere on the sea of love.

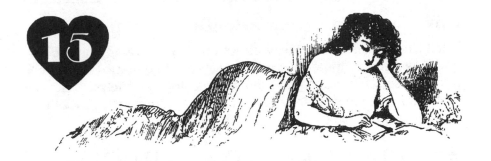

Erotica— Novel Tease

THE PLOT QUICKENS . . . (PANT, PANT)

It was a dark, cold November night. The windows inside the pick-up truck were steamed. Still Emma Sue could see Billy Ray's raging hard-on. Pulling his zipper down, she gasped as fourteen inches of throbbing manhood sprang forth, stiff and straight. The firm, round head was moist and glistening. He moaned as she put her hands around the shaft, barely able to fully grasp his enormous rod entirely. Emma Sue's heart raced wildly and shivers surged through her body. "Take me, before I perish!" she pleaded.

He entered her moist, virgin opening and filled her to the very depths of her being. Emma Sue was afire. A flood of love juice poured out as she climaxed thirty, forty or more times (who could count?) Billy Ray waited until she was satiated before erupting like a volcano, spurting forth rapturous rivers of fluid in unending, powerful jets. They rested mere minutes before starting an even more sizzling round two.

Now That I Have Your Attention

Hard to believe? Not in the world of erotica where anything goes and everyone comes, 'n comes. A steamy scenario starts you thinking sexy and soon you fantasize playing out the part. As the plot thickens, your pulse quickens and, you know the rest of the story . . . or do you?

What's Black, White and Read All Over? Erotica!

"Sexually explicit" is today's term for highly descriptive erotic material, although raunchy reads have been around for ages. Ancient cultures produced erotic art, drama and literature. In fact, the word *erotica* comes from "Eros," the name of the Greek god of erotic love. Writings on the old walls displayed that the Greeks had more than one word for **it**. Hieroglyphics found in the pyramids depict overtly sexual acts. From what I viewed touring the ruins in Italy, the gladiators diddled and Nero fiddled around long before Rome burned. Hot times in the old towns haven't really changed, and passionate plots basically remain the same. Only the names and places have been altered to protect the not-so-innocent. Thankfully, the fascination for erotica will endure forever.

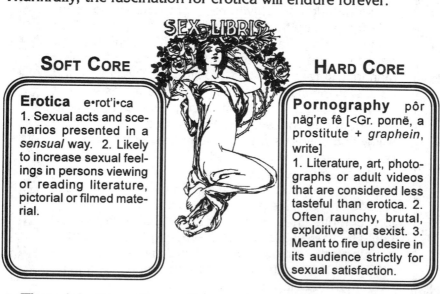

SOFT CORE

Erotica e•rot'i•ca
1. Sexual acts and scenarios presented in a *sensual* way. 2. Likely to increase sexual feelings in persons viewing or reading literature, pictorial or filmed material.

HARD CORE

Pornography pôr näg're fê [<Gr. pornë, a prostitute + *graphein*, write]
1. Literature, art, photographs or adult videos that are considered less tasteful than erotica. 2. Often raunchy, brutal, exploitive and sexist. 3. Meant to fire up desire in its audience strictly for sexual satisfaction.

Though both words are often used interchangeably, sales show that most women prefer erotica and the more sensual material it covers . . . and uncovers, too!

```
 EROTIC STEREOTYPES

All males are: 1) lean, mean, love machines; 2) strong, last
long and are, of course, larger than life; 3) muscular, brave,
powerful, hot and handsome; 4) ready, willing and oh so able
for Mable, Betty Grable or even Clark Gable.
All females are: 1) ageless, agile, adorable sex kittens, over-
endowed, over-sexed; 2) forever ripe 'n ready to climax at the
opening of a zipper; 3) novel bimbettes who never fake it be-
cause they're mega multi-orgasmic; 4) never bitchy from PMS,
hot flashes, headaches or the heartbreak of psoriasis.
```

Take It Clitorally, Not Literally

Since literary license is used to keep the reader randy, erotica can
be misleading, as the following illustrates:

In reality, **real** women are real happy with one, or at best, a
handful of orgasms. When they occur, it's catalysmic to be sure,
but actually the earth doesn't "move". . . neither do some of the
women (you out there know to whom I'm referring!)

Novel Teasers and Pleasers

Erotica's all around and sales keep soaring. *Playgirl* and *Woman
on Top* are popular female versions of *Penthouse* and *Playboy*,
commonly referred to by men as "one-handed" or "stroke"
magazines. These and similar publications geared toward female
readers are available at newsstands, convenience stores,
pharmacies and supermarkets. Erotic books, sex manuals and
how-to's are found in psychology, health or relationship sections
of book-shops. Hard-core porn abounds at adult bookstores or
can easily be mail ordered. Be prepared to shell out a pretty penny
for industrial strength raunch. However, package deals containing
back issues can save big bucks. They're usually bundled three for
the price of two but the content's never outdated since the
outcome's always the same. Then, as now, an orgasm is an
orgasm, is an orgasm.

Buy Lines

Even with the sexual revolution behind us there's still a stigma
attached to females publicly perusing and purchasing adult

material. Men think nothing of openly drooling over their favorite centerfold, yet slyly stare at us liberated women shoppers. Perhaps they feel we're invading their private territory, as was the case when females started buying condoms. If you want to save the hassle and embarrassment, treat yourself to a skin slick subscription or membership in an adult book club. All year you'll lap up those hot buns and stories too. Personally, I changed my attitude and take my sweet time scanning the latest issues of *Honcho* and *Inches* (my favorite all-male magazines). At $5.00 plus, why leave lust up to chance? I make darn sure to get my money and honey's worth.

Lusty Library Lends

Shhhh . . . You're entering the public library. Are you aware some libraries stock a liberal selection of erotica? True, you won't find XXX-rated porn, however, many books once "banned in Boston" are now shelved openly. For starters, check sections #301, #613 and #823. *Books in Print,* found at the reference desk, lists by title or category most everything published on sex or any subject.

On Borrowed Time

There's no need to buy a steamy read. Here's a partial list of erotica you can borrow. Check out these favorites:

Classic Erotica ☑

☐ *Delta of Venus* (Anais Nin). The first modern erotic book by a female author that's still hot stuff.

☐ *Little Birds* (Anais Nin). Thirteen torrid yet tender seductive stories.

☐ *Cheri* (Colette). From sex to strawberries 'n cream, an older woman initiates her young lover into delights of the senses.

☐ *Fanny Hill* (John Cleland). Bawdy tales featuring Fanny's pranks and good parts, including, but not limited to, her famous fanny.

☐ *Lady Chatterly's Lover* (D.H. Lawrence). A nobleman's wife romps with the gardener who royally trims her bush.

☐ *The Pearl* (Assorted authors). Vignettes, Victorian poems and short stories about sex in 'daze' gone by.

□ *Tropic of Cancer* (Henry Miller). A journey into a man's soul that continues to his loins and the sexual hot spots of the woman he worships.

□ *Portnoy's Complaint* (Philip Roth). Amusing and arousing true confessions. While dreaming of making love the author masturbates. When making love, he wishes he were masturbating. (Sound familiar?)

□ *Endless Love* (Scott Spencer). Stripped of clothes and inhibitions, the characters endlessly engage in sizzling sessions.

Erotica Not Always Found in Libraries ☑

□ *Story of O* (Pauline Raeage). A woman's fantasy of dungeons and torture in a French mansion. An exciting story for those who aren't into pain, but enjoy fantasizing about it. Full of humiliating ceremonies that whip you into shape without vulgar language.

□ *Alida* (Edna MacBrayne). Entertaining, exciting and well-written novel from the perspective of a modern woman who's middle-aged (whatever that means).

□ *I Am the Beautiful Stranger* (Rosalyn Drexler). A lusty heroine makes sex fun and games. (Isn't that what it should be?) A nice antidote to male authors who present female heroines as sexually passive and submissive.

□ *Candy* (Terry Southern and Mason Hoffensberg). Candy is dandy as a sweet pubescent who not so innocently carries on with many men, including but not limited to her gynecologist and guru.

A Collection of Fantasies ☑

□ *Secret Garden* (Nancy Friday). A ground-breaking book that stirs mind, body and soul. Overflowing with dozens of women's true erotic fantasies written to send your erogenous zones soaring.

□ *Forbidden Flowers* (Nancy Friday). The author does it again with even more fantastic fantasies indulged in by libidinous ladies with lustful liberated minds.

□ *Herotica* (Seojie Bright). A stimulating variety of twenty-one short stories by wanton women more than willing to share their frenzied fantasies.

How-To's that Lend a Helping Hand ☑

Besides being bawdy and *beducational*, erotica **can** increase sexual savvy. Much is written to teach you about your body, new positions and fun for two or one.

☐ *The Sensuous Woman* ("J"). A landmark book when introduced that playfully and sensibly encourages masturbation and opens a Pandora's box full of sensual fun. This all-time blockbuster was my introduction to self-pleasure. Too bad it wasn't published sooner . . . all those missed orgasms, darn!

☐ *Touching for Pleasure* (Kennedy and Dean). A beautifully written and illustrated book on enhancing sensuality through the language of touch.

☐ *Sex for One* (Betty Dodson). An artist of masturbation who teaches solo sex in a down-to-earth, practical manner.

☐ *The Joy of Sex* and *More Joy* (Alex Comfort). Covers and uncovers everything erotic in an illustrated, informative, easy-to-read style.

Pillow Books

Add state-of-the-art arousal to sexual solitaire by feasting your eyes on a "pillow book"—the term for erotica containing very graphic and sensual illustrations of sexual postures from various cultures.

Library Lends

The Erotic Arts (Peter Webb)
Erotic Art of the East and *Primitive Erotic Art* (Philip Rowson)

Not in All Libraries

Loving Couples (Hokusai)
Perfecting Erotic Passion (Rudiger Boschmann)

Not satisfied with these library picks? Don't despair—many more selections are available. If you're not into borrowing but prefer building your private collection, read on for provocative possibilities.

Question: What's entertaining, super hot, fun between the sheets and comes monthly?

Answer: Adult Magazines!

They contain articles, advice and lots of naughty but nice nude centerfolds for every body's taste, fetishes and fantasies.

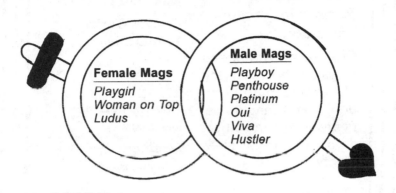

Female Mags
Playgirl
Woman on Top
Ludus

Male Mags
Playboy
Penthouse
Platinum
Oui
Viva
Hustler

Mini-Magazines

Risqué-r 'n friskier mini-sized monthly adult publications contain lusty letters, *ream-y* reads, nude and lewd photos, intriguing illustrations.

☐ Penthouse Forum
☐ Letters
☐ Turn-on
☐ Human Digest
☐ Real Letters
☐ Erotic Mail

Raunchy Referrals

Name that fetish—bondage, same sex, cross-dressing, foot fetishes, swinging, rubber, spanking, S&M, whips and, whew, what have I overlooked? Pick and choose from a wide variety of adult publications catering to specific sexual preferences. Available at adult book stores, select newsstands or through mail order.

XXX-Rated All-Female Magazines and Books

Growing by high-heeled leaps and bounds is the all-female market of books and magazines. Peruse these and others if you're into chicks-a-plenty.

Magazines

On Our Backs
Yellow Silk

Books

Bizarro in Love
(Jan Stafford)
Leading Edge
(Lady Winston)

All-Male XXX Magazines

"So many men, so little time." Who said there's a man shortage? Not so, if you hop in the sack with an all-male magazine. Just as guys are turned on by erotica portraying a bevy of female beauties, women are aroused by magazines displaying men doing their own thing themselves and to one another. Although targeted at homosexual males, these publications offer juicy jump-starts for

Magazines
❏ *Honco*
❏ *Inches*
❏ *First Hand*
❏ *Jock*
❏ *Mandate*
❏ *Stallion*

Books
❏ *Adam*
❏ *Bayou Boy*
❏ *Boys of Brazil*
❏ *Black Gold*
❏ *Fox Hunt*

many a female. Even if you don't care for whips, leather, tattoos, etc., some of the stories and pictures are worth a thousand orgasms!

Paper Capers

Here are some neat and discrete ways to store erotica and get to the good parts pronto:

- ♥ Use stick-on notes to index steamiest, dreamiest sections instead of wasting time searching for them.
- ♥ Clip out pictures of favorite nude dudes and slip them between the sheets (of clear plastic, that is). Then place your rouges gallery in a ring binder or folder marked "Horny Hunks."
- ♥ Snip stories and info that will quicken your pulse. This eliminates stacks of magazines, saving space and precious time thumbing through pages looking for Mr. "Write." When a lewd mood strikes, you can roll into action with your favorite characters.

. . . and the Plot Continues

In the opening story, Emma Sue was completely crazed with lust. Could it be Billy Ray was really "that good," or had Emma Sue previously been inspired by grossly exaggerated erotic books or magazines? Read some raunch and find out

> ### CLEAN UP YOUR ACT
> Remember: recycle magazines you're tossing; give them away or work out an exchange system with a friend.

what your racy reaction is. Recite the most passionate parts aloud and picture yourself as the literary *lithario*. See your guy as a hero, big wheel or heck of a heel. Devour tantalizing tales to unleash unbridled passion while Billy Ray, Rhett Butler or the butler himself leads you to orgasms, happily ever after.

Fantasy— Good Head Trips

Welcome to Fantasy Land

Can I interest you in a great getaway? A dream vacation? Jet to Hawaii and get the lay of the land (and your sex life, too) or lie low in Soho. You can have all the lusty adventures you want, anywhere, any way, with anyone you desire . . . No infection, rejection or restrictions apply. Hold it, you don't have to get packing or leave home. This is an out-of-this-world flight of fancy, and the ocean liner, limo or Lear jet leaves as soon as your thoughts take off. Sounds too good to be true? It's not!

Think a Good Game

Once upon a time it was believed only men fantasized sexually. We now know better. Studies reveal two-thirds of all females fill up their pretty heads with fantasies. Like masturbation, fantasies are rarely talked about or shared because we think friends or lovers will either disapprove, or get the idea we want to act them out. Truth is "nice" gals do indulge in raunchy as well as romantic daydreaming. Does that make them wanton women? No way. Imagination can be whimsical, wild and whatever; it's the stuff that builds thrilling novels when in actuality many authors live only mundane lives.

Females who enjoy sexual fantasies tend to have lengthy, detailed ones and do them up in style, whereas males usually concoct wham-bam-thank-you-m'am encounters. Either way, mind games are escapes that can instantly and magically transport you on a voyage of voluptuous dreams.

POST CARD

HAVING A
WONDERFUL TIME
...PRETENDING
YOU'RE HERE
XXXooo

Mind/Body Connection

Sexual stirrings begin in the brain and may have a powerful effect on bodily responses. A hot fantasy may get a man erect in as few as twenty seconds. With women, the reaction causes vaginal tissue to swell and lubrication to start. Soon the entire system is aroused. Since it's impossible to grasp two thoughts simultaneously, allow your mind to fabricate some eexcitement. Immersed in a satisfying scenario, it's impossible to worry about bills or that old bugaboo, "Will I climax?"

Fantasy and Me

I love fantasizing. Whether in bed, stuck in traffic or doing dishes, a fantasy a day keeps me wanting to play. If a guy catches my eye, automatically I wonder what kind of lover he'd be (bet you do that, too!) The content of my daydream depends on how attractive I find him. Inventing a hot plot always gets me in the mood and keeps me focused, especially during solo sex. So much so I don't think I'd reach orgasm or enjoy climaxing nearly as much without one. I'll let you in on a little secret. In reality, I'll take romance, candlelight, slow seduction and all that schmaltzy stuff. In the world of make believe, my mind harbors a hint of depravity . . . yeah!

Truth or Consequences

Don't be a travel agent for guilt trips—give yourself permission to fantasize. It's perfectly normal and natural. If you have difficulty letting your imagination run rampant, take the following mini test. Answer *true* or *false*:

T	F	
___	___	Women who have their sexual act together don't need fanciful daydreams.
___	___	Nice gals never get ideas like *that*.
___	___	Your fantasies reveal your true nature.

The answer to all three questions is a resounding **false**. "With'it" women realize provocative dreaming is healthy and liberating. There's only risk if you feel compelled to act the risqué ones out. Squelching fantasies may inhibit complete sexual enjoyment. If the *idea* of being a prostitute or princess for a night is exciting to you, give it a whirl. Who's to know? Start thinking a good game. Enough said. Pack up your guilt, ship it off to Timbuktu, and immerse yourself in a secret saga of choice.

Dreams for Sale

Need a nudge putting your imaginary itinerary together? Are the same fantasy faces and places getting too well trodden? Even the most exciting scenarios can become undervalued if overplayed. Take the easy route to arousal: Beg, borrow or buy a sex-capade from *Women on Top, Playgirl* or other publications. For more adventure, try *Forum for Couples*. Read movie or soap opera magazines and rub more than shoulders with the rich, famous or infamous. Get swept off your feet by the hero in the latest best seller. Be whisked into a hedonistic rendezvous with videos or a favorite celeb. You're the tour director—travel your way!

Do I Dare Share?

Now that you're ready to embark on a mind-boggling excursion, bet your wondering if it's okay to bring along a travel companion. The decision of whether or not to share your fantasies with a partner is touchy. Perhaps he'd love hearing yours and delight in sharing his with you. Perhaps your fantasies might make him jealous or suspicious wondering if you want to enact them. Check it out by reading erotica together then discussing the story. Listen for subtle or overt clues of encouragement or disapproval. While doing this, sit or lie close to one another. Another tactic is reading letters printed in the "Reader Asks" section of *Penthouse*, *Playboy* or a similar magazine. Not only do they get you talking about sexy topics, but they'll tickle your hot spots, too.

How Awful . . . Awfully Good I Mean

Getting kidnapped, ravished by bikers, or being disciplined are surprisingly the #1 fantasy turn-ons for many females. Other popular themes are orgies, obedience and orgasms galore. Let's not forget voyeurism, exhibitionism and water sports. Unlike reality, where even the lustiest sometimes experience sexual frustration, in fantasy, everything's fantastic. You're mistress or, if you prefer, master of your destiny. Your mind can conjure up a grabbag of *goodies* and *baddies* and the choices are endless. Jump start your imagination and get playfully motivated with this fantasy match game.

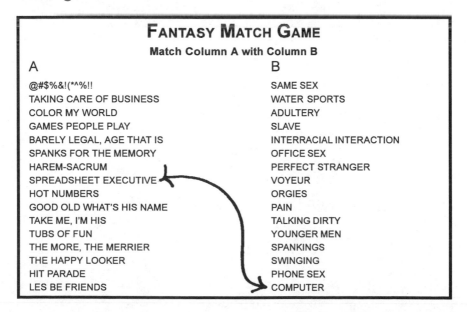

FANTASY MATCH GAME
Match Column A with Column B

A	B
@#$%&!(*^%!!	SAME SEX
TAKING CARE OF BUSINESS	WATER SPORTS
COLOR MY WORLD	ADULTERY
GAMES PEOPLE PLAY	SLAVE
BARELY LEGAL, AGE THAT IS	INTERRACIAL INTERACTION
SPANKS FOR THE MEMORY	OFFICE SEX
HAREM-SACRUM	PERFECT STRANGER
SPREADSHEET EXECUTIVE	VOYEUR
HOT NUMBERS	ORGIES
GOOD OLD WHAT'S HIS NAME	PAIN
TAKE ME, I'M HIS	TALKING DIRTY
TUBS OF FUN	YOUNGER MEN
THE MORE, THE MERRIER	SPANKINGS
THE HAPPY LOOKER	SWINGING
HIT PARADE	PHONE SEX
LES BE FRIENDS	COMPUTER

Booking Your Trip

Numerous publications dealing with fantasies are readily available at the local newsstands. These unreal stories can really inspire sexual desire. One or two tales may be all it takes, but avid adventurers keep a well-stocked libido lifting library. This primer lust list can get your engine going. Climb aboard and head straight-away to the *sex-perts* at Romantic Antics Travel Agency.

GET ON THE RIGHT TRACK WITH ...

Romantic Antics Travel Agency

Quickie Fantasies
My Secret Garden
Forbidden Flowers
Men in Love

Novel-Tease
Xaiv. Fant. Sex
Fair Oaks
Delta of Venus

Magazines
Playgirl
Erotic Mail
Intimate Letters

PHONE: 800-FAN-TASY

THE ROMANTIC ANTICS TRAVEL AGENCY

and their sizzlin'

FANTASY TOURS D 'LAMOUR

Sex-cessfully planning an imaginary itinerary is our goal. Much care, creativity and thought goes into each tour to provide you with peak thrills. Romantic Antics has many years of *expert-tease* in the far-reaching field of fantasies. Our clients are assured of being in the right spots and always having enough time to linger and enjoy. Picture indulging in all the mild or wild romps you've ever desired. Feel secure you're in competent hands.

Prepare to be aroused, entertained and seduced with one or more of our erotically charged trips. Choose from a host of amenities and activities guaranteed to make the time spent mesmerizing and memorable. You absolutely can't go wrong choosing a never boring or routine *tour d'amour.* If you're not 100% satisfied at any point, transfer out and slip into another destination, no questions asked. That's why, when it comes to fantasies, the savvy traveler escapes with a Romantic Antics tour. Quite frankly, no other travel agency will do.

Relax, we take you in style. Your first-class get-away is designed for the solo sightseer; however, there's no additional charge for sharing. Each trip encourages you to fill in the blanks and customize your imaginary itinerary. Stay and play as long as you'd like, going back 'til you've had your fill.

Choose a trip from these popular themes or include your secret schemes. Here's the passport to paradise. Proceed at your own speed.

☐ Seduction ☐ Domination
☐ Swinging Partners ☐ Exhibitionist
☐ Condom Control ☐ Traveling Saleswoman

PASSPORT
United States of America

Plan ahead as you would for a real trip. Allow adequate time to see the sights, do the delights . . . or have them done to you. Before ETD (estimated time of desire) reserve time and dress or undress properly or improperly. Set the mood with candles, incense, traveling music, a "bon voyage" glass of bubbly, then get comfy. Here are additional tips to lift your spirits and get you off without reservations:

- Don't check X-rated baggage (for example, toys, joys, etc.). Have fantasy "fuel" handy during layovers—videos ready to roll and erotica propped and opened to the juicy parts. To enhance your joyride, playthings should be accessible, plugged in or charged.

- Avoid getting sidetracked. Concentrate by blending fantasy with feeling. Stroke yourself while imagining your dream lover's tongue, hand or other appendage doing this and especially that!

- Never impose limits. Once into your fantasy, let naughty notions flow. There are no "off-limits" ideas. Some of the silliest scenarios provide the best endings.

- Travel lighthearted, but enhance your mindful meandering with props suitable to your *emotional climate*:

  1) Stranded on a tropical island with a suntanned stranger? Using a large scarf, drape your body sarong style. Enjoy the sensuous feel of the fabric caressing your skin.

  2) Snowbound with a fair-haired ski instructor? Picture yourselves sprawled naked on a bear skin rug. While doing so, stroke your body with a flurry using something furry.

  3) Ready for an evening in gay "Paree"? Don your spiked heels and mesh stockings with garter belt.

- Parlez-vous Français? Hablo Español? #@$%^&!!!? Talk a good game, too. Verbalize down'n dirty words in whatever language you prefer with your pretend paramour. Don't just think it, verbally beg or demand, "C'mon Jacques/José/ Joe! Fill my very depths." Tell him, "Do it now, oh yes . . . harder . . . faster . . . ahhh!" Moan, groan and gyrate as if he were actually there.

❤ On extended *sexcursions*, keep it kinky but keep the kinks out by moving around. Don't make it a laid-back layover; instead of simply reclining, roll over onto your tummy and hoist those sexy buttocks high. What a way to come in for a landing.

X-plore l'Amour with a Sizzlin' Tour, or One Personalized by You

It's time to get playful. Close your eyes allowing your mind to float off to a fantasy Island, solo or with a make believe mate. Teasingly draw the trip out with feeling and finesse. Don't rush

Tour #1: Seduction

Fantasized by: **Margie**

Ca$h 'n Carry: Ahhh, sweet seduction, where the scenarios focus on the slow and gentle art of taking possession or being possessed. Fly to Monaco for an evening casino excursion where your charms captivate a visiting oil sheik. You enticingly persuade him to jet you to Verona, Italy. There by moonlight, in the Roman Arena, under Juliet's balcony, you seduce him out of 100 gushing orgasms and a $10,000,000 endowment.

Self-Guided by: _____
                              (your name)

Love Thy Neighbor: You're home alone, and since it's sweltering, you remove all your clothes. Your neighbor's college-bound son stops in to say good-bye. Forgetting you're naked (sure, sure) you invite him inside. The bulge in his pants doesn't go unnoticed. He's young and innocent. You shouldn't, but can't resist reaching down to_____. He can't control himself and responds by___. The visit is spent_____ .

TOUR #2: TRAVELING SALESPERSON

Fantasized by: **Chastity**

Clothes Encounters: On the road again and it's been a productive week. You're anxious to get home but the flight doesn't leave until 8:30 PM. Since it's only 1:00 you stop by the hotel lounge for a bite of lunch. The waiter brings over a cocktail from a handsome hunk at the bar. You signal him to join you. He's also in sales, introducing a new line of ladies lingerie. The attraction is mutual as eyes meet and sparks fly. He accepts the invitation to bring samples to your room for a private showing. Your heart pounds wildly, as you take off his business suit, surprise, surprise . . . macho Freddy's wearing a frilly teddy. What a fashion understatement he presents!

Self-Guided by: _____
(your name)

Monkey Business: What luck! While on a boring business trip you meet a marvelous looking man in the hotel elevator. He asks, "What floor?" "Yours," you reply, hoping he'll_____. Once in his room you cast all caution to the wind and_____. Wow, whee! How could you know he'd have a huge_____and adore_____. You want more, so the perfect stranger obliges by_____. Finished, you begin showering, he follows and____. Finally dressed to leave, he hands you his business card, and with a wink you reply_____.

Tour #3: Swinging

Fantasized by: **Prudence**

Scrabble® 'n Dabble: Every Friday night your best friends join you in a hot game of Scrabble. To keep things interesting, you've initiated "theme night," where extra points are scored for words pertaining to the targeted topic. Last week's theme was "Perversion." Jill came dressed as a dominatrix and Jack,  the flasher, was nude under his raincoat. Your well-hung husband John played voyeur; you were a sex food addict (heavily armed with plump hard bananas and, of course, whipped cream). First Jill and John scored big with the word *spanked* worth 95 points. Soon after, Jack and you triple creamed them with *orgasms* worth 225! The playfulness led to a celebration and a mad scramble to the bedroom where everyone teamed up and came out winners!

- -

Self-Guided by: ＿＿＿＿＿＿＿＿＿
(your name)

Who's Boss: The boss invites you to a dinner party. Across the crowded living room your eyes meet and lock. His wife is no where to be found, neither is your husband. You plan an escape to a guest bedroom. Once inside, in the darkness you passionately＿＿＿＿＿＿＿. Unable to control the lust, he ＿＿＿＿＿. You're both starked naked before realizing his wife and your husband are＿＿＿on the floor. The four of you get hot for each other and＿＿＿＿. Your husband wants you to＿＿＿＿. You want to see him＿＿ her. Both men want to . The other woman is into＿＿＿＿. Since then, this frenzied foursome has＿＿＿＿.

Tour #4: Safer Sex

Fantasized by: **Rachel**

Teachers' Pets: You've volunteered to teach **safe** sex courses in adult education. The class of ten male students have involuntarily been sent to school because they refused to wear condoms during intercourse. After giving them the scary statistics on STDs, you proceed to explain the benefits of mutual masturbation as a pleasurable  alternative to intercourse. Your breasts spring forth as Jason dutifully unbuttons your blouse. At your command, Steve removes your skirt and hoists you onto the desk. You instruct the students to remove their pants and start stroking their penises. Ted happily volunteers to vibrate your clitoris as directed. Every classmate is erect and attentive as you offer your hot love box to the first "Juan" to don a condom. To your amazement they all line up and anxiously wait their turn to spring into action!

Self-Guided by: _____

(your name)

Condom Sense: Mike is the sweetest honey you've met in a long time. Tall, handsome, broad chested, sporting a great set of buns to boot or____! In preparation for your first night of sex, you've bought flavored condoms and have been practicing putting them on a cucumber, using only your mouth. As anticipated, Mike arrives and starts _____. Horny and hot, he begs you to_____. "Not without a condom," you insist. He refuses until your tongue seductively_____. He can't believe how it _____. You promise to____next time. He wants you more than ever and_____.

Tour #5: Exhibitionist

Guided by: **Penny**

Auto Erotica: Ambassadors, corporate presidents and visiting royalty rent limousines. As owner of your own limo service, you offer exceptional options to discriminating travelers. One wealthy client insists you're personally in the limo that picks him up every afternoon. On the slow ride through Beverly Hills, you intoxicate his senses with unmentionable deviant delights. He yearns for the days you bring a well-endowed male or female friend along (your choice). His favorite turn-on is having you stand stark naked in the open sunroof, while he #$%^&!!* you from below. Weekly he lavishes you with diamonds and other expensive trinkets. It's a business doing pleasure with him, and naked, you're laughing all the way to the bank!

Self-Guided by: _____

(your name)

Never a Board Meeting: Your billionaire boyfriend loves when you're naughty 'n nasty in public. "Sugahhh Daddy" showers you with furs, Ferraris, five hundred dollar bills and_____ .
Showing appreciation, you surprise him at his corporate office dressed in five-inch heels, a full-length sable coat and_____.
"Daddy's" in a board meeting. You barge in and fling off the coat. To "Sugahhh's" delight you_____. The men watching begin to _____. Dancing on top of the cherry wood table you start _____ then_____. The climax comes when_____.

TOUR #6: DOMINATION

Guided by: **Joy**

No Pain, No Gain: You believe in sexual equality, or, better yet, female domination. In your rhinestone choker, black leather teddy, spiked boots and cat-oh-nine-tails whip, you're a formidable, pulse-quickening, heart-wrenching sight. Unashamedly biased towards female superiority, you treat men as obedient hungry pets. Groveling at your heels they beg for approval and punishment. You'll have none of their wimpy ways and proceed to whip them into  submission . . . . ouch! Like animals in heat, with tongues and other parts hanging out, they keep coming back for more.

- -

Self-Guided by: _____
                              (your name)

Whipped Dreams: Your breasts are adorned and dripping with silver chains. The black thong bikini accentuates your round, firm, fully packed derrière. You look like a sex kitten as a cat shaped sheath slightly exposes your glistening pubic hair. Pointed black-studded boots fit snug and hug your shapely  thighs. There's a _____in your hand ready and waiting for that naughty man to arrive. Right on time, he knocks at the door and, once inside, hands you_____. You order him to remove his clothes and bend over the chair. He begs you to_. Again and again, harder. Pleading, he _____. You allow none of that. Now in a lusty frenzy, he _____.

Slowly open your eyes and float back from that secret place. Hopefully you've savored every heavenly sensation your mind, body and spirit could conjure up. You had it all . . . for a brief but "wonder-full" moment. Until next time, kiss your special someone and your fantasy good-bye. ***The best is yet to come!***

Whisper in my ear,
I'll follow you anywhere.

Telephone Turn-ons—
Getting Good Phone

Dial-a-Hunk

Home alone and want to add sizzle to sexual solitaire? Here's a turn-on right at your fingertips, as close as your phone. Accessing special 800 and 900 hot lines, you can reach out and touch someone while touching yourself. With the growing need for **safe** sex, Barbara's, Beth's and . . . Belle's are ringing as women increasingly plug into this popular self-pleasure pastime.

Sexually Speaking

This business of phone sex isn't new. For years, men have been dialing up racy conversations and listening in while a sultry-voiced female verbally seduces them with their fantasy of choice. As a result, countless men receive an earful as well as a handful. With the advent of cordless, cellular and speaker phones, satisfied customers are keeping lusty lines ringing and cash registers jingling.

Recently, females have been given equal *eartime* with woman oriented phone sex companies. Calling hunk hot lines enables us to listen in while a guy, gal, or combinations there of, sweet talks us into fantasy land (hopefully orgasm, too) using a theme of choice. Simply supply charge card info, then ask and ye shall receive. Talk as much as you want, or you have the right to remain silent.

Broad Appeal

In order to entice more females to use phone sex services, some companies conducted a survey to ascertain what women wanted to hear. Psychologists were employed to help plan a feminine format. The results: melodic male voices, rhyming words, soft background music. Messages are less graphic, more seductively romantic than those used for male callers. Other companies provide dialogue that's down'n dirty like those for dudes. Another distinct difference is cost. Female hot lines are half the price of male services. Is that because we *take* . . . whoops, *talk* longer?

Information, Please

I called a few female phone services (strictly for research, mind you). Finally getting through to one New York City number, I heard their phones ringing like crazy in the background . . . and it was almost midnight. The smooth operator who answered claimed his company dishes out dialogue so sexy they warn women. "Call, but be ready to blush at what our men say . . . then tell only your most liberal-minded friends about us." (That's **you**, isn't it?)

Reaching out for more information, I called a nationwide California service and questioned the head honcho. In response to my questions, he claimed his company stopped using pre-recorded messages since most women preferred speaking with live wires. He added that his service receives 40,000 calls a month . . . now that's saying a mouthful. Continuing on, he described the tools of his trade and proudly informed me of being able to serve up phone fantasies much like fast food. I couldn't help but think, next time I'm hungry for a hunk, I'll order in my ring-a-ding Romeo with soft buns and a nice big pickle . . . yummy!

Phone Sex Doesn't Come Cheap!

Directory Assistance

As popular as these companies are, they may be here today and gone manana (like some of my real-life relationships). Check current adult publications such as *Playgirl* or alternative news-papers for updated listings.

Time flies when you're having fun, and since phone sex chatter isn't cheap, learn to listen, talk, then react rapidly. At $2.00 plus per minute, every phone moan and groan counts. In other words, skip the foreplay—this may call for a quickie. To speed things up, keep vibe handy, or your credit card may end up with a bigger charge than you.

Lay It on the Line

With approximately 10 million AIDS carriers and the number of victims growing rapidly, safety conscious sexual swingers are becoming smooth operators. Using speaker phones and three-way calling, couples make appointments to hook up together and get kinky. The buzz word for this *ménage à phone* is "earbanging" and their motto is "Hang up your hang-ups cause anything goes." A single woman wanting to get on-line involved with this non-physical connection can find the numbers of ready listeners in swinger magazines. Although you can't reach out and touch someone physically, your number will be up for grabs. When phone-a-vision and virtual reality become affordable, *earbangers* will be banging down the doors to purchase them.

Mating Call

A nationwide phone message system is the latest service to hit the singling 'n ting-a-ling scene. For a monthly fee, sexy voice mail companies assign subscribers a private code accessing them to an electronic voice message exchange. Engage a good ear and hot little finger to . . .

- Receive personal messages while maintaining anonymity.
- Talk to anyone within the system, receive your own voice mail message or simply lay back and listen to torrid talk.

- Pre-record your proactive pearls of wisdom and enticingly introduce yourself to new callers.
- Make contacts using a supplied directory of ready listeners.

With everyone's privacy assured, callers can say whatever strikes their fancy or fantasy. Telephone timid? Listen in with one ear and get only half as embarrassed.

"Hi, this is Barbie. I'm a tall buxom blonde with magic fingers and luscious slender legs I'm just *thighing* to wrap around your body . . . Leave your message at the tone and . . . "

Ears Looking at You, Kid

Don't have a date or a steady Freddy? Is it because you: 1) Can't do a thing with your hair? 2) Have nothing to wear? or 3) wouldn't dare get bare?

Ears the solution . . . get yourself a phone pal? Similar to pen pals, they're heard from but rarely seen. If this type of relationship appeals to you, place an ad in the personal section of your local news, singles or alternative lifestyle paper.

CALLERS WANTED

Strictly for phone sex. No charge, commitment, or communicable disease!

Discourse minus intercourse is safe, satisfying yet very sexy. Read the response one southern Belle got from her ad.

ROMANCING THE PHONE

Once upon a dime, a ringer named Belle had a long distance phone affair with Bill, a pro quarterback. At least once a month, he calls his gal and the conversation goes something like this:

Bill: "Hi sweet stuff, this is your monthly Bill. Did you miss me?" Just hearing his voice gets Belle tingly. They make small talk, and before long the conversation turns steamy, burning up the wires.

Bill: "I wish I was there kissing, caressing and licking every inch of your bodacious body."

Belle: "Is this an obscene call?"

Bill: "It is, and I want to run my tongue up and down inside your soft thighs. Would you like that?"

Belle: "Ohhh baby, yes."

Bill: "Are you wearing panties?"

Belle: "Ah, ha . . . and they're getting wet."

Bill: "Take them and anything else off." Without hesitation, Belle gets naked.

Bill: "You know I love your huge hooters; squeeze them for me."

Belle: "I wish you were here to lick my swollen nipples and #@!$%^&*+!!!"

Bill: "Since I'm not, play with yourself and tell me everything you're doing."

Belle: "Okay, but first do something for me. Pull your pants off and fondle yourself."

She knew he was making a connection to his throbbing erection. His breathing quickened along with hers as they described every erotic, neurotic move. Soon both are unable to speak, and only moans, groans and heavy panting can be heard. After a short pause, they giggle at what's been pulled off. More than once Belle has said, "I love being his call girl and getting my quarterback, too." Bill exclaims, "Mah Belle gives the best *aural* sex in town." Doesn't that have a certain ring to it?

To Coin a Phrase, This Is One Phoney Story! But Yours Needn't Be . . . Get the Message?

Off the Record

What happens if you don't have a significant other to give you good phone? Use a handy-dandy tape recorder and do it yourself. Here are some suggestions to plug into:

- Call a sexy service and tape the conversation for instant replay later when the mood strikes.
- Record a tape while reading erotica then replay it while playing with yourself.
- Ask a male friend to read some raunch and record tapes for your listening.

XXXtra User-Friendly

Computer circuits are on-line and sizzling with sexy come-ons . . . (so that's what those nerds have been cooking up). Spicy computer bulletin boards are a call away using your PC modem—I've heard that 9000 *bods* [bauds] are better than 1. Numerous free services allow you to download at no charge and get a large charge with erotic public domain software. Numbers are available through the "grapevine" of PC enthusiasts in your area.

Advertised in some PC magazines are software dealers offering X-rated board games, high-resolution pictures and talking movies. If you play around with multi-media and purchase a lusty laser program, boot up and look closely at the bottom of your monitor. Barely visible are teeny-tiny phone numbers to call for a hot bed of sexy data. Get lucky and maybe you'll find the spreadsheet executive of your dreams on-line in his favorite lotus position.

Getting Good Phone

Listen up . . . here's how to be on the receiving end of phone sex. Before dialing, set a steamy scene:

- ❏ Have music playing softly in the background.
- ❏ Lower lights and burn a candle or incense.
- ❏ Dress in something sexy, sleazy or nothing at all.
- ❏ If available, use a cordless phone, or one with a speaker.
- ❏ Sip mineral water, tea or wine.
- ❏ Gather an inflatable doll, blindfold, love oil, favorite hunk picture, feathers, boots; in other words, whip up lots of imagination.
- ❏ Have joy toys on tap and ready to get buzzing; if asked what the noise is, blame it on the connection!
- ❏ Know what fantasy, theme or fetish you want and be prepared to ask for it—this is your dime so don't hold back.
- ❏ Wear a watch or set a timer to go off **after** you do.
- ❏ Remember, time is $$$, honey.

Above all, hang up your hang-ups. If this doesn't get you tingling on the telephone, perhaps you've reached a wrong number.

CLICK!

Video—
Sex, Sighs
and
Video Tapes

A Reel Turn-on

What's a high-tech turn-on that can, at the press of a button, switch on sexuality? Adult videos, of course. These movies can ignite flames of passion in men and, contrary to common belief, women too! This is evidenced by the increasing numbers of adult flicks females are snatching up. For private and partnered viewing pleasure, plugging into XXX-plicit erotica does more than entertain. It can do the following:

- ☒ Get you hot when you're not.
- ☒ Educate as well as beducate.
- ☒ Show a partner your willingness to experiment.
- ☒ Open your mind (and legs also) to new ideas.
- ☒ Teach sexy ways to dress and undress.
- ☒ Enhance solo or shared fun and games.
- ☒ Gets you psyched up about using toys, ploys and new positions.

TURN-ONS

Additionally, watching the action tempts, teases and encourages us to act out our fantasies. Many women nix viewing for some of these reasons:

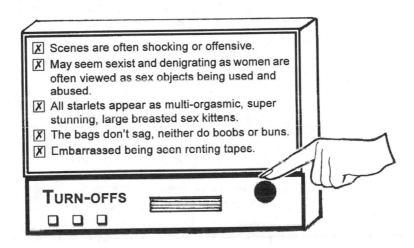

- [X] Scenes are often shocking or offensive.
- [X] May seem sexist and denigrating as women are often viewed as sex objects being used and abused.
- [X] All starlets appear as multi-orgasmic, super stunning, large breasted sex kittens.
- [X] The bags don't sag, neither do boobs or buns.
- [X] Embarrassed being seen renting tapes.

TURN-OFFS

Adult videos are written erotica "come alive" and may not be for the faint- hearted. So they don't have any redeeming values, who cares! Your deepest fantasies can be played out without having a heavy date, dressing up, or applying blush (although you'll have plenty to blush about). Before dimming the lights and letting 'r roll, here's a crash course on how to electronically charge up solo sex.

Feature Comforts

Now that the gear's affordable, versatile and user-friendly, thank goodness, VCRs are as common as TVs. The good news for non-mechanical females (me, me) is VCRs are a cinch to operate. This means you won't need a handyman to help you tune in and turn on. Sure, it would be swell having one around, but, trust me, you can handle this job yourself.

If shopping for a VCR and confused by the options, use the KISS principle: **K**eep **I**t **S**imple **S**weetheart. The less you have to fiddle with, the more time you'll have to diddle.

Buttons and Beaus

A feature no video viewer should be without is a remote control. Now that I have one, I'm no longer jumping out of bed to re-run the good parts causing climax interruptus. My state-of-the-art VCR lets me control the action to suit my mood of the moment. I simply hit a button to start, stop, slow the torrid action or search for a favorite steamy scene. With a remote, you can easily direct a private showing from the comfort of your bed, couch, or "sleazy" chair.

Power On—Button, button, you've got the button that turns the machine one and you too!

Play—Dim the lights, get toys 'n joys ready, press and aaaction.

Power Off—That's all folks . . . tune in tomorrow for another XXX-citing episode.

Stop—Interrupts play and flips picture back to TV. A quick trick to use in case someone suddenly walks in.

Mute—Turns off sound allowing you to get hot and bothered without action, without being overheard.

Pause/Still—The pause that refreshes.

Rewind—Re-play it again, Samantha. See the coming and going and the going coming.

Fast Forward/Scan—Get to the good part by passing ho-hum turn-off parts of dippy dialogue, ugly sheets and butts with pimples 'n dimples.

Sleep Mode—Had enough fun sleeping beauty? No problem, the VCR can be timed to shut off automatically.

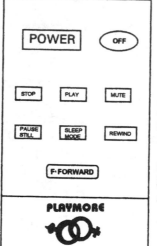

Subjects at Hand

There are literally millions of XXX-video viewers and thousands of flicks to tempt every taste. Films cover everything from *Accouterment* to *Zippers* in three basic categories: soft core, hard core and self-help.

Since taste in movies as in everything else varies, view different categories and see what stirs things up for you.

Welcome to Sex "1 Ohhh 1"

To pick up a few new turn-on tricks from adult flicks, feast your eyes on educational tapes. These are available for singles and couples wanting to discover their full sexual potential, solo or shared. Motivational movies are passionate without being perverted and risqué without raunch. Here are a few videos to get you going:

Approved Videos by the Broad of Education

Better Sex Video Series: Experts teach techniques for enjoyable foreplay, intercourse and using adult toys.

Sex for One: Betty Dodson, artist and advocate of masturbation, shows a group of women how to become orgasmic.

Strip for Your Man: Learn to teasingly grin and bare it all.

How to Love Your Lover: Explores the Zodiac in romantic ways.

Playboy Sex Videos: Ploys and joys to up your sexual savvy.

Sex After 50: Dr. Lonnie Barbach conducts explicit interviews on menopause, erection and other topics with people ages 50-90.

My Body's My Business: Prostitutes give the lowdown on **safe** sex and demonstrate putting condoms on with your mouth.

In addition, use your VCR to view tapes on exercise, make-up, health, nutrition and personal development. Feeling, looking and

thinking good in all areas of life are interrelated and can, unequivocally, assist you in becoming a fully sensual woman.

Keep an Open Mind, Eye & Thigh . . . Oh My

If you only watch romantic films where women are wowed, wooed and won, Candida Royalle of Femme Productions produces softer porn with music and a romantic story line. This for-women, by-women market is evocative, provocative and well worth looking into. Experiment with varied subject matter. View a flick where the female is sexually assertive. Perhaps she's getting it on with two men (lucky lady), two gals with one guy (lucky fella), or one where the femme fatal is a domantrix displaying her tricks while men grovel at her feet, before working their way up. Keep an open mind and you might be astounded at what presses your hot button. I rented the entire raunchy gamut and discovered my favorite turn-on is all-male videos starring a stable of sun-tanned studs. The sight those hard bodies in action never fails to keep my undivided attention.

Be Reel-istic

A word to the wise *videophyle*: true the plots leave much to be desired, but this isn't the time to play Siskel and Ebert. Simply look between the lines (loins, too). Don't compare yourself or a partner's physical attributes or performance to what's going on or coming off on screen. In adult films, boobs are always round, firm and fully packed; buns are tiny, tight and toned. Women wallow in wondrous amounts of wet, wild orgasms, and hunks are well-hung and always ready, willing and able. In these sizzling scenarios, no one ever says: "Ouch, that hurts," "Stop, you're messing my hair," or "Not tonight dear, I've got housework, a headache or halitosis."

Everyone enthusiastically hops into the sack, the pizza delivery boy delivers stuff hotter than pepperoni and cheese and the next door neighbor borrows something sweeter than a cup of sugar. The actors break into sex the way athletes break out in sweat, and

they do every imaginable thing—some unusual or hilarious, a few educational, and others, yuck-ohhh! True, there may be a lack of plot justification, but the performers do their best to appear making it rather than faking it. (Aren't we all capable of being academy award winners in *that* category?)

Tapes on Tap

At $2.00 plus, renting adult films can be a **safe** and spicy way to spark up sex. Note, you won't find porn at all video outlets, but many independently owned stores stock enough of a perverse selection to keep you coming back. If you're looking for super smut, frisky foreign or fetish flicks, use mail order or raunchy stores. To find convenient outlets, look under "Video Rentals" in the *Yellow Pages* and let your fingers do the stalking. Call and inquire:

- What types of explicit XXX-rated videos do you rent or sell?
- Is a membership fee, credit card or cash deposit required?
- What is the cost per day? (Some places offer special deals; for example, 3 days for the price of 2, half price on certain days, etc.)
- Is there a senior citizen discount?
- What are your store hours, and do you have an after-closing drop-off?

What's Behind the Green Door?

Although women are watching XXX-rated tapes in increasing numbers, the adult section of video stores remains predominately a man's world. Most look like converted broom closets tucked away in a remote corner. It's not the sign, warning "You Must Be Over 21 to Enter," that stops most women. Nor is it the flimsy fabric hanging to conceal the "debauchery" inside. As with purchasing erotic magazines and adult toys, some women feel intimidated entering a pseudo male domain. If truth be known, many men are just as embarrassed. To make matters worse, videos aren't categorized, so it takes time to browse. Wouldn't it be great if stores offered XXX-rated film catalogs to "wannabe" watchers so women could walk up to the counter and order by number? Any store owners out there listening?

The Movies and the Shakers

Don't be mislead thinking the title bears or even *bares* any resemblance to the movie it's supposedly portraying. For instance, the hype on the cover of a cassette entitled *A Streetwalker Named Desire* will unlikely be like the original screen classic, *A Street Car Named Desire*. Often the pretty people plastered on the box never make it to the ball, except for a cameo appearance. Once familiar

A PORN STAR IS BORN—HOLLY

"I guess you could say I was a slow starter entering the sex scene. Even though I thought about **it** a lot, I was concerned about **safe** sex and finally had my first experience at twenty-three. Ron and I met and dated in college. One night after graduation, he invited me to his apartment to watch a movie. Much to my surprise it was XXX-rated. I was intrigued and couldn't believe people were actually doing many things I'd only fantasized about. Ron watched my mounting excitement and it wasn't long before we made love. Since then we've been living together and make viewing adult videos a regular happening. Monthly we decide on a theme such as leather, lace, light bondage, etc. After collecting props, we watch a porno flick correlating with our plan. Occasionally, I'll strut my stuff dressed as a streetwalker in garter belt, mesh hose and an awesome pair of spiked heels. Believe it or not, sometimes the shoes are literally on the other foot . . . his! I'm getting so good at acting, who knows, one of these days you may see a porn production starring me, *Holly Wood* . . . and I would if I could."

with certain porn stars, you'll have a better idea what to expect in their videos. Rent a few films at a time and increase your chances of lucking out with one that's awfully exciting rather than just awful. Since there's much to choose from, if at first you don't *sex-ceed* rent, rent, again.

Take a tip from Holly and don't just lay back and watch the randy rompings. At least some of the time get involved by fantasizing or playing the part. Act celeb, dress up or down as a nympho nurse, French maid, town tramp-ette, etc. Be both voyeur and star until your own grand finale.

Show, Tell and Share If You Dare

Have a partner and want to discover his sexual preferences? Let him choose a video then hand him the remote. Does he replay boobs, butt and bondage footage or fast forward to lap-up oral sex scenes? Be aware, and you'll get a picture of his secret desires. If you're hesitant about telling him what you prefer, take the remote and press on watching his reaction. He'll get the hint. Don't worry if you discover he's turned on by something that makes you want to hide under the covers. Hold back criticism. Once you get over the shock, you'll be delighted he shared his hedonistic hankerings. For the most part, when the film ends, so do bizarre thoughts.

Compile a Video File

Now that I'm big on video viewing *of all types*, I've devised a neat way to keep track of movies I've rented or own. Using a small five-column bookkeeping pad, I jot down info on tapes bought, rented or lent.

Video Title	Rented/Bought or Loaned to	Date In	Date Out	Subject Matter	Comment or Not
Better Sex	Own	5/12/92		Couple shows how	Mom should see
Insati-ble	XYZ Video	8/10/92		Chambers best	Behind the eight ball

Blockbuster Orgasms

With the availability and versatility of adult videos, there's no need to frequent singles bars searching for a Sly, Burt or Clint look-alike. Go ahead and indulge in intimate interludes with John (10-inch Holmes) or Jeff (Swell-Hung Striker). They're ready and waiting to be invited into your boudoir. True, the "reel" thing's not for real, yet these private showings may be the ticket to box office orgasms. Go ahead, pop in a flick but pass on the popcorn. Hopefully your hands will be *bedder* occupied!

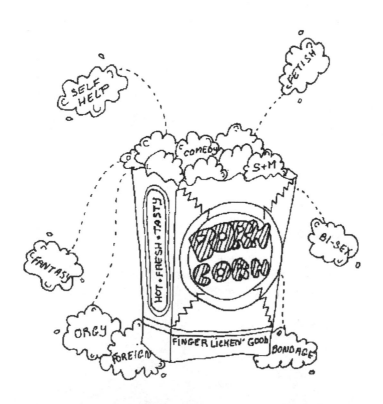

Buy,
Try,
Sigh—
Babes in Toyland

Shop Talk

"Born to shop," "Shop 'til You Drop," "So Little Time, So Many Malls"— what woman doesn't enjoy shopping? Aha, not a hand went up! Well, there's shopping and there's *adult-R-rated* shopping. Concerning the latter (even today) many women would rather stand naked in front of a firing squad than walk into an adult toy store. I know how intimidating **it used to be** and, until recently, I also felt uncomfortable. Now with upbeat boutiques rather than off-beat raunchy stores, I sincerely believe a woman's place is not only in the White House and the mall, but sex shops as well. Let's check out what's in store.

Please, No Sleaze

Not long ago, sleazy adult bookshops were the only places to find provocative playthings. These stores were situated in neighborhoods not bragged about by the Chamber of Commerce. Staffed and frequented by an unsavory array of men, understandably few females ventured inside. If they mustered up the nerve to enter, they found items displayed in intimidating ways. This caused many a disappointed shopper to hot-foot it out fast, empty-handed, never to return. Had they stayed long enough and gotten past more bizarre items, they would have discovered an extraordinary array of adult toys.

A TRUE STORE-Y

"The first time I got courage to go sex toy shopping I had trouble finding a female friend to accompany me. When asking my main squeeze, surprisingly, this so-called macho male flat-out refused. Being determined, I begged, pleaded then promised a "reward." He grudgingly took the bait and off we went, with me practically dragging him. Our outing took us to a raunchy sex shop on a dark street in lower Manhattan. We entered, trying to act non-chalant, but lost our cool upon encountering black walls displaying dildos the size of dinosaurs, whips, handcuffs, masks and nipple clamps (ouch). I started to back out but my friend beat me to it. In order to avoid his "I told you so," I stayed, keeping my head bent, certain other customers were watching my every move. I was too nervous to realize they probably were embarrassed as well and didn't want to be seen either.

I stayed a tortuous ten minutes, then left with sensual oil, a dildo that squirmed and some bawdy books for my "hero" whom I hoped was still waiting in the getaway car.

Years later, the dildo remains a friend *in*-deed but, unfortunately, I can't say the same for the guy who left me in the lurch that eventful evening. Oh well, win some, lose some!"

A Store Is Born

Unfortunately, tacky places still survive discouraging many women from buying erotic accouterments. The faint-hearted needn't despair. Less sleazy shops have come to the rescue. To passers-by, specialized boutiques may look strictly like lingerie shops. The names, however—Sassy Cat, Lace To Lust, Love Lace, etc.—teasingly hint that there's more in store than feminine finery. Along with crotchless panties, condoms and a cache of lingerie, these less explicit erotic emporiums sell tempting toys and joys. Some stores display sexy items openly; others adhere to occupational codes and keep them behind the counter, or in "adults only" back rooms.

You might be pleased to know, newer adult boutiques are often staffed and owned by women, making it comfortable for you to browse and ask questions before buying. One such store in New York City called Eve's Garden is adorned with feminine touches, and only allows men if accompanied by a woman. Now, more females are frequenting these boutiques and business is booming.

No Frills Thrills

You may be surprised to find that many drug, department and discount stores offer a convenient way to purchase playthings. In some major malls, gag and novelty emporiums stock a sampling of adult toys. For many years pharmacies have carried scalp, back, and ever-popular phallic-shaped "facial" massagesr. All are supposedly sold strictly for therapeutic purposes, however, we know better.

Plug-in and battery body massagers abound in discount and department stores. Find them openly displayed alongside hair blowers and small household devices. Snoop around and with luck you'll discover a multi-attachment model. To appear therapeutic, this body massager is pictured with a model soothing his/her aching neck or back. Although garden variety vibrators aren't packaged with more intriguing sexual attachments as those from adult sex shops, they get you humming at half the price, with no reduction in arousal.

Speak Easy

Too timid to ask outright for a vibrator? Then request a body massager for your aching muscles. You don't have to convince the clerk you've got a bum back by wearing a brace or stooping over. Besides, the pleasure this device brings is sure to last long after any embarrassment ebbs. Still hesitant? I'll lend you my Groucho Marx mask. The nose, mustache and glasses will obscure your true identity.

No Place Like Home

Home is where the heart is and by far it's the coziest place to purchase playthings. No, not TV's Home Shopping Channel, although that may be the next sexy sales frontier. I'm talking toy buying à la home party plans. These get-togethers are a terrific way to tactility and tastefully check out playthings before making your selections. Here's how this party hearty plan works.

7:30 PM: *Ding-dong.* The salesgirl arrives and sets up a display of her company's goodies.

8:00 PM: The invited women anxiously arrive and are handed pencils, order forms and product brochures.

8:15 PM: Bring in the icebreakers. Laughter, levity and a little lascivious game playing begins.

8:30 PM: The atmosphere has changed from apprehensive to adventurous as the inquisitive buyers become attentive listeners. The representative does a show 'n tell of the "softwear/hard ware" she's brought along.

9:00 PM: Time for a refreshing pause—a hands-on closer look at the merchandise and personal ordering off in a private area.

10:00 PM: Smiling faces hurriedly head home clutching little brown goodie bags.

11:30 PM: Missed the late night news cause something more important came up . . . I think we have another satisfied customer!

HOME TOY 'N JOY PARTY
No Men Allowed

Pleasers 'n Teasers

Hot sellers on the home party front are sexy lingerie and love lubricants. Hottest moving product remains electric and rechargeable vibes.

Interested in having or attending a sexy toy party? Check the following:

- ✔ Classified ads in newspapers, listed under business opportunities.
- ✔ Call and inquire at lingerie, adult novelty and sex boutiques.
- ✔ Look in "free press" and alternative type newspapers.
- ✔ Check ads in the back of some savvy women's magazines.
- ✔ Visit franchise or women's trade shows.

Stamp Out Embarrassment

Still haven't shopped for adult toys? Is that because you have . . .

- ❤ No need.
- ❤ No one to share them with.
- ❤ No time.
- ❤ No . . . um, nerve?

No more excuses! Without stepping a sneakered or sling-backed foot out the door, you can purchase X-rated gadgets, gizmos and gimmicks. Simply mail order sexy stuff to save time and avoid embarrassment. Though merchandise may be a pittance more pricey, buying this way is discrete and convenient for shoppers who are tempted but timid.

Ad-vantages

Flip through *Playgirl* or any of the more suggestive magazines and you'll see ads galore for X-rated accessories. Although they may be referred to as "marital aids" don't let that archaic term deter you. To entice buyers, many companies offer descriptive catalogs for a nominal fee then deduct the cost from your first order. Be aware, most of these full-bodied brochures leave little to the imagination and in themselves could be a turn-on. To assure privacy, catalogs and your selection(s) arrive in the proverbial plain brown wrapper.

Satisfaction Guaranteed?

Most adult mail order companies deliver merchandise that's at least a reasonable facsimile of items depicted. No matter how tempting a toy, try dealing with established companies such as Good Vibrations, Xandria, Adam and Eve, and Stamford Collection. These merchants repeatedly advertise in popular magazines and offer a satisfaction guarantee if items don't perform as promised. (Wish some of my dates came with this guarantee!)

Pick a Card, Any Card

If possible, charge purchases, then if something goes wrong, credit card companies can help you obtain a refund or replacement. The post office assists if merchandise is undelivered or fraudulent, but, let's face it, it's embarrassing to describe a lost sexual device or one that's a dud. Even liberated me would have trepidations telling a postal inspector, "The 12-inch dildo didn't measure up," "The inflatable male doll had a deflated ego," or "The vibrator didn't *hummm* my song."

Buy, Baby, Buy

That about wraps up this toy shopping segment. Don't dilly-dally any longer. Make your list, check it twice, then plan to buy some things naughty but nice. Ready, set, go-o-o-o . . . hey, wait for me!

Vibrators— SeXercises for Every Body

Babes a Buzzin'

What's this? You've got an out-of-shape, saggy, draggy, sex life? Has the fear of contracting a **S**exually **T**ransmitted **D**isease put your libido on lapse? Well, wait a liberated minute—this is the decade of personal fitness. To keep yourself in top shape a *total* workout is required. This means exercising your mind, bod and yup, sexuality, too. What you don't use you lose! No need to panic—we aren't talking killer crunches, vigorous burn your buns-off or hum-drum routines. Quite the contrary. We're suggesting pow-pow-power packed "work-ups" that are dynamite solutions for even laid-back ladies. Without Jane Fonda, jumping-jacks . . . or Jack himself, get into high gear by turning on with *Sizzlin' SeXercises*.

Pleasure You Can Measure

No Partner? No Time? No Orgasm? We're advocating no sweat, instant results. Young graduates, youthful seniors and women of all ages are discovering regular sexual workouts go the distance to:

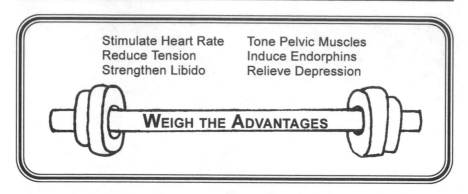

Stimulate Heart Rate   Tone Pelvic Muscles
Reduce Tension   Induce Endorphins
Strengthen Libido   Relieve Depression

WEIGH THE ADVANTAGES

In addition, this specialized body work increases circulation and excitation. For superb, self-pleasure body shaping, Sizzlin' Sex suggests a sensational, yet simple piece of equipment—a *vibrator*. You know, that device advertised to "ease muscular pain." Sexually speaking, they're unequaled for activating orgasmic muscles and putting **you** in control of a knock-out sex life. These lean, anything but mean, machines are **safe**, easy to use and provide championship results. Best of all, there's no risk of infection, rejection or exertion. Is it any wonder that aerobically and erotically there's a whole lot of shaking going on?

Gear, Gadgets 'n Goodies

Fast-paced fitness classes, back-aching weightlifting or boring stationary bikes aren't included in our program. Shed sneakers and designer body gear, too. Your wash 'n wear birthday suit will suffice. With vibe in hand you'll know why countless women continuously enjoy vibrators for:

- ♥ Speedy sexual pick-me-ups
- ♥ A perfect "10"tion reliever
- ♥ Getting and keeping them in the mood
- ♥ Increasing orgasmic response
- ♥ Adding verve and versatility to solo or shared sex

Convinced? Great, then 1) commit to taking care of the inner (sexual) as well as the outer (physical) you, and 2) exercise your right to satisfying sex, whether or not you have a hard body buddy to work out with.

To determine your present level of sexual fitness and discover the merits of our power-packed program, fill out the *Sizzlin' Sex* Membership Form. You have lots to gain, zilch to lose (except an inhibition or two).

Sizzlin' Sex
Sexual Health & Fitness Membership Application

Our Invitation:
Free lifetime membership extended to _____ (*your name*). Husbands or playmates always welcome to share workouts.

Our Commitment:
To design a sexual health and fitness program that's **safe**, sensual, satisfying and anything but routine. Guaranteed positive results.

Program & Hours:
Select from state of the he♥rt *seXercise* machines, then play at your own speed. Open 24 hrs, 7 days a week including holidays, conveniently accommodating your busy schedule. Routines performed in the privacy of your home—no classes, crowds, competition, or cop-outs.

Basic Requirements:
For a tantalizing total body work-up, determine your current level of sexual fitness. Choose your program, gear and goals, then jump right in. But first, complete the following questionnaire, circling applicable answers.

| **Age:** | Under 30 | 30-49 | 50 - 64 | 65 - 105 |

| **Stage:** | Single | Married | Widowed | Divorced |

Orgasmic Quotient: Score
0 - No Desire   1 - Never Orgasm   2 - Sometimes   3 - Multi Orgasmic

Goals:	Score 1	Score 2	Score 3
	Feel Sexy	Control Response	Fine Tune Skills
	Learn to Orgasm	Increase Libido	Mutual Masturbation
	Reduce Tension	Create Excitement	Increase Orgasms

Add Score and Determine Sexual Fitness Level
　　　　0 - 4 Beginner　　5 - 8 Intermediate　　9+ Advanced

Maximize your potential and achieve peak performance with one of the following high-tech devices.

Dream Machines

Vibrators fall into three categories: strap-ons, multi-attachment and wands. Some are stronger, longer or offer interchangeable attachments, but all add muscle to solo or partnered playtime. Flick a switch and receive constant stimulation—whenever, wherever, forever! The continuous rhythmic throbbing is so satisfying, it usually provides non-orgasmic females a first-time climax. You can bet it won't be their last . . . enough said. Side-step the mechanics and move to the dynamics, starting with Swedish massagers.

Swedish Massagers

How Swede Is It?

Electric vibrators made their debut at the turn of the century. First on the scene was the Swedish or scalp massager, a real heavyweight which took both hands of a masseuse to maneuver. Technology rapidly improved, size decreased and barbers began treating customers to neck and scalp massages. (Could it be that barbershop quartets formed to sing the praises of this device?) Naaah!

Yankee ingenuity being what it is, libidinous ladies (and men, too), discovered that moving the appliance from their heads to more erotic parts delivered stimulation that made more than hair stand on end. Word spread, sales soared and mechanical masturbation came of age. Scalp massagers remain popular because they keep the user involved by transmitting pulsations through the hand and fingers to places touched. Unfortunately, you'll have to play fast, as these heavy devices tire hands quickly. Although in the running, sexually they don't finish first. Why take our word for it? Shake loose and feel for yourself.

How to Have a Strapping Good Time

- Slide hand under straps allowing finger-tips to do the walking and sensual stalking.
- Touch tingly fingers to scalp, slide on shoulders and arms then encircle breasts with whisper-soft strokes.
- Using pulsating palm, foray a path to your belly gradually trailing onto the sensual fold where leg joins torso.
- Massage outer hips, buttocks and backs of legs continuing down to feet. Return up inner leg, lingering around upper thigh until primed for pleasure.
- Glide quivering hand atop genitals massaging entire love area. Use fluttering fingertips to fiddle with clitoris.
- Place heel of vibrating hand on pubic bone while lightly stroking labia lips. Vaginally insert index finger of same hand, keeping a throbbing thumb on clitoris.

Lean, Mean M-M-Marvelous Machine

Multi-attachment vibrators go to the head of the class with many a lass and might win the most applause . . . if our hands were free long enough! These vibes are, by virtue of their attachments, the most versatile. Use them to massage everywhere: back, buns, scalp and shoulders, including, of course, **all** your erogenous zones and, surprise, surprise . . . even his! These awesome appliances, masquerading as body massagers, are up for grabs at drug, discount, department and surgical supply stores. A real honey for little money as they are:

- Dual speed.
- A cinch to handle.
- Lightweight yet pack a wallop.
- Whisper quiet, minimizing distraction and insuring privacy.
- Equipped with interchangeable attachments that provide dynamic workouts, inside and out.

Most multi-attachment massagers come with four latex tips, *not intended for internal use*. Shape determines the degree of flexibility and whether sensations are focused, intense or subtle. Unfortunately, instructions included with most vibes are erotically deficient. In order to keep abreast of general as well as genital massage workout possibilities, here are a handful of hints plus quips on tips.

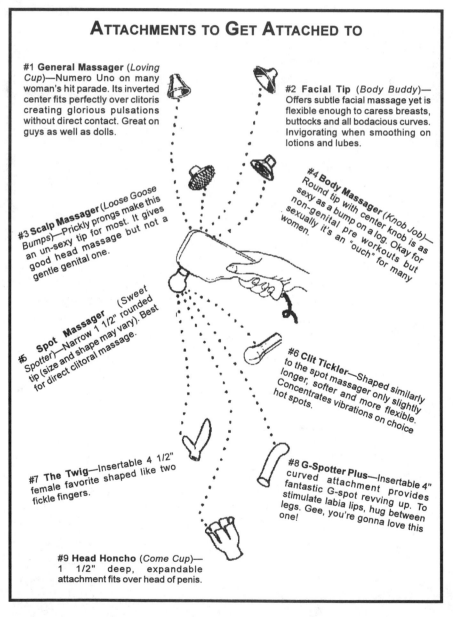

ATTACHMENTS TO GET ATTACHED TO

#1 General Massager (*Loving Cup*)—Numero Uno on many woman's hit parade. Its inverted center fits perfectly over clitoris creating glorious pulsations without direct contact. Great on guys as well as dolls.

#2 Facial Tip (*Body Buddy*)— Offers subtle facial massage yet is flexible enough to caress breasts, buttocks and all bodacious curves. Invigorating when smoothing on lotions and lubes.

#3 Scalp Massager (*Loose Goose Bumps*)—Prickly prongs make this an un-sexy tip for most. It gives good head massage but not a gentle genital one.

#4 Body Massager (*Knob Job*)— Round tip with center knob is as sexy as a bump on a log. Okay for non-genital pre workouts but sexually it's an "ouch" for many women.

#5 Spot Massager (*Sweet Spotter*)—Narrow 1 1/2" rounded tip (size and shape may vary). Best for direct clitoral massage.

#6 Clit Tickler—Shaped similarly to the spot massager only slightly longer, softer and more flexible. Concentrates vibrations on choice hot spots.

#7 The Twig—Insertable 4 1/2" female favorite shaped like two fickle fingers.

#8 G-Spotter Plus—Insertable 4" curved attachment provides fantastic G-spot revving up. To stimulate labia lips, hug between legs. Gee, you're gonna love this one!

#9 Head Honcho (*Come Cup*)— 1 1/2" deep, expandable attachment fits over head of penis.

Experiment and merriment with all the accessories, but **never, never** insert any attachment not specifically designed for **in**-*ternal* affairs, or you may make the headlines in tomorrow's tabloid.

NATURAL IN-QUIRER
X-CLUSIVE REPORT

Mystery Woman Gives Local Doctor a Hot Tip

Date Line: West Palm Beach, FL
Department: Lust 'n Found

Early Tuesday morning, "Frannie"* awoke feeling frisky and started using her vibrator. Caught in the throes of auto-erotic ecstasy, she did a NO-NO and vaginally inserted the general massage tip. Thrashing about with pelvis pumping caused the attachment to pop off and land up her "wazoo." Try as she might, Frannie couldn't retrieve the tip. Needing a helping hand, she nixed the idea of calling 911 and fled instead to her doctor's office. Entering red-faced, she remained flushed and flustered while he probed around, finally retrieving the elusive accessory to the crime. Hurriedly paying the bill, Frannie exited quickly, minus the attachment (she was too embarrassed to ask for it). I wonder if medical insurance covered that visit . . . it was, after all, an accident.

* Her name's been changed to protect the gyrating gal . . . and me, too! She threatened to strangle me with a vibrator cord if her true identity was exposed!

 *Wand Massagers*

Wand-er-lust

Searching for another means of magically revitalizing your workout? Try a *wand* vibrator. Originally introduced as a deep muscle massager, these machines have rapidly been upgraded to a high performance adult toy. Before you can say "hocus *pokus*," wands produce provocative pulsations throughout flexible rounded heads and provide enchanting full-body excitement. See why they're on many a maiden's wish-list.

A wand's length helps to reach out and erotically touch yourself further than multi-attachment models. Other knock-out advantages this sensuous spellbinder offers are:

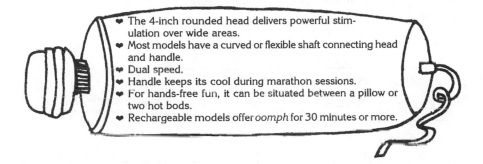

- The 4-inch rounded head delivers powerful stimulation over wide areas.
- Most models have a curved or flexible shaft connecting head and handle.
- Dual speed.
- Handle keeps its cool during marathon sessions.
- For hands-free fun, it can be situated between a pillow or two hot bods.
- Rechargeable models offer *oomph* for 30 minutes or more.

The following accessories fit snugly over the wand's head:

 G-Spotter. Curved to probe (your) G-spot or (his) prostate. With mega maneuvering, there's no chance of attachment falling off.

 Multi-Attacher Tip. Enables you to pop on multi-attachment vibrator tips. Superb for reaching sexy sites too small for wide wand head.

Popular brands to charge up with are: Hatachi Magic Wand, Oster Rechargeable Stick Massager, Bodymate by Homedics and Sunbeam Stick Massager. Buy, try and discover how waving a wand stirs up real magic.

WARNING???

Before starting this *seXercise* program, check vibe making sure it's fully charged. Sizzlin' Sex isn't responsible for lack of orgasm due to power loss!

Wand Workouts

The following chart describes bewitching *seXercises*. Choose and use a few or mix this regime with others mentioned throughout the book. Keep your sexuality in optimum shape for a lifetime by working out 3 times weekly. Okay, twice a week. All right, how about once a week! Make it 3 sets of 8 reps each.

Body Position	Wand Position	Wanderful Routines
Lying	Hold lightly over clitoris	Brush surrounding area, pressing, releasing, circling as you go . . . and come, too!
Lying, knees bent	Two inches over genitals	Raise hips, tighten PC and rotate against wand. Relax, lower pelvis.
Lying down	Over puffy pubes area	Gently squeeze mons with hand, raising it against pulsating head. Roll pelvis, release, relax, repeat.
Kneeling over vibe	Secure on pillow	Move up, down and around on wand then hold on labia for 10 counts.
Kneel (doggie style)	Move from pubes area to perineum	Stroke inner thighs, labia lips and clitoris. Great position for partner play as he'll feel pulses within your throbbing love tunnel.
Lying, legs outstretched and together	Gently press against mons	Tighten legs, flex toes back and forth. Swivel hips while circling wand against pubes. Lift vibe, playfully teasing libido.

Play It Again, Samantha?

Why stop after the first orgasm when you can keep sensations flowing as long as you want? If clitoris gets hyper-sensitive, place palm over it with vibe on back of hand. Relax, breathe deeply and rhythmically while gyrating pelvis. In minutes, clitoral supersensitivity should be replaced by renewed responses that might provide yet another orgasm. This is a super-duper exercise to help you become multi-orgasmic.

"And the Beat Goes On . . . " Ta Da

Assorted vibrators go the distance to keep work-ups from being anything but boring. With many different models to choose from, no doubt you'll find one that suits your style.

- Think two heads are better than one? Hitachi offers an ultra powerful, double-headed wand that's especially exhilarating when hugged between a gal's or guy's upper thighs. Many men reel over the feel their penis receives as it's stroked between the two vibrating heads.

- Try a 3 1/2-inch powerful, portable plaything called G-2 (among other names). The nubby head offers incredible vibrations with one AA battery. Under ten bucks it's a nifty gift for those wanting one more for the road . . . an orgasm, that is.

- Hatachi's 5-inch Mini Massager is discreet and neat for tension-free traveling. Three changeable tips lightly nip and nuzzle via one C battery.

- Calling all land lubbers and hot tubbers. Pollenex offers a gentle waterproof work-up with their battery-powered Aquasagger. It comes with three go-with-the-flow tips usable in pool, shower, sauna and so forth.

The Heat's On . . . But Why Sweat It?

Some vibrators offer a heat feature; however, save your cold cash. While warmth works wonders on sore muscles, it's not so hotsy-totsy for masturbation (unless you live in Alaska). Regular massagers get you hot enough, mama.

On the subject of hot topics, some manufacturers caution that electric vibrators used 20 minutes or more might overheat. While we've never experienced this, for prolonged simmering sessions, consider using two vibes. Alternating them lets the machine, not you, cool down. **If a new massager gets hot after a few minutes, return it.** It's a dud.

Choosing the Purr-fect Plaything

Many massagers that look alike aren't created equal. Though it's not possible to intimately try before you buy (would you want to?), here's how to get the feel, if not the thrill of it all:

1. Is vibe comfortable in your hand?
2. If the store lets you plug it in or provides demos, check vibrations by moving tip against hand then up arm.

3. Notice noise emitted. It should whisper sweet hums; dental drill drones are out.

4. Check stimulation at each setting opting for a more powerful machine. Then, if necessary, use atop fabric or clothing, getting used to pulsations (which won't take long).

5. Check tips for snug fit so they won't pop off before you.

Besides being healthful and sexually helpful, vibrators provide years of trouble-free titillation. Most report having a long, meaningful relationship with their marvelous massagers without a broken part, heart or trouble of any sort.

Maid for Pleasure

For germ warfare and your welfare, clean up your act—and accouterments after **each** use.

- If removable, pop off attachment, wash with mild soap, then rinse.
- Wipe vibe and accessories with rubbing alcohol making sure liquid doesn't seep into mechanism. Dry.
- Substitute pre-moistened towelettes for quick toy clean-ups, when traveling.
- Unfortunately, with today's **safe sex** concerns, extra care is essential when sharing playthings. Sex shops now offer Adult Toy Cleaner containing Nonoxynol-9 for added protection.

Smart Belles: Here is some sexy stuff you've read a zillion times before, but what the heck. If you are serious about shaping up your sex life, do at least some of these:

- ✔ Make time for self-pleasuring. Eliminate unnecessary distractions.
- ✔ Vary positions, ploys and toys.
- ✔ Be playful, give your pulsating plaything a name.
- ✔ Activate your body—don't let the vibe do all the work.
- ✔ Personalize routines; verbalize and imagine yourself with a real lover.
- ✔ Use music, soft lighting, arousing videos, or fantasy.
- ✔ Alternate time, place and routine when with a partner (if you have one).
- ✔ Keep your sex drive alive by pumping pleasure on a regular basis.

Basic Fitness Levels

Beginner

Using a vibrator for the first time? Expect an orgasm! If you don't get one, enjoy the feeling anyway. **It will happen** the 2nd, 3rd or 103rd time. Resuming after a period of abstinence. (Is that possible?) Go for the gusto and gold, too!

5	♥ Use slowest speed for low impact work-ups. If necessary, wear panties to minimize vibrator sensations.	5
L	♥ Add sensual oils and give yourself a full-body massage.	L
B	♥ Work out using wand routines or multi-attachment suggestions in Quips on Tips.	B
S	♥ Stick with it. Soon you'll advance to another level.	S

Intermediate

Are there areas of your sexuality that need pumping up? For example, do you climax too slowly, irregularly, or not at all? No big deal. Here's how to overcome these obstacles.

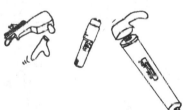

10	♥ Dynamic equipment is essential. Compare your vibe with other brands making sure it's powerful enough.	10
L	♥ Do suggested *seXercises* adding your personal touches.	L
B	♥ Explore genital area while watching reactions in a mirror.	B
S	♥ Get in the mood beforehand. Wear garter belt, sexy underwear, crotchless panties or no panties at all.	S

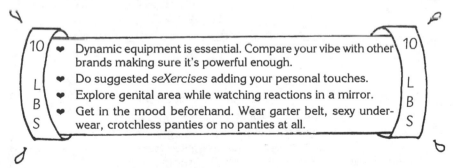

Advanced

Challenge yourself, giving it your all, using high impact equipment, and really focusing in. Add to toy collection with various vibes and dildos. Once you've confidently mastered

using them, invite a playmate in to see what's buzzing. Woo him with feminine wiles and seduce him with your fantastic fun stuff. Blame only yourself when he keeps coming back for more.

20 L B S

- ❤ Elevate endurance. Start, stop and enamor yourself before climaxing.
- ❤ To become multi-orgasmic, go back and reread "Play It Again, Samantha."
- ❤ Add self-penetration to jubilation using a dildo.
- ❤ Vibes offers 100% **safe** mutual masturbation.

20 L B S

World class orgasmic stars are made not born. They capture the winning edge because they've worked at achieving perfect moves while correcting weak spots. If they can do it you can too.

See **ya** in the winners circle!

Very Personal Programs

Who wants to waste time on programs that fizzle out? Read the following profiles and see what positive results other woman experienced.

Name: Marianne   **Age:** 39 & holding

Marital Status: Divorced

Children: 3   **Profession:** Bank Supervisor

Profile: I lead a healthy lifestyle by eating well, taking vitamins and exercising regularly. Being single, I make sure to keep sexually fit by masturbating several times weekly. It keeps me content until Mr. Right comes along.

No Sweat Routine: Using a rechargeable wand vibrator, I'll lightly circle my clitoris going from side to side, top to bottom, until unable to bear the ecstasy one more minute. I prefer letting arousal ebb and flow making the resulting orgasm so overwhelming, I rarely want a second one.

Name: Lyla   **Age:** 60+

Marital Status: Widowed

Children: 3   **Profession:** Retired Nurse

Profile: Volunteer work, family involvement and the threat of STDs keeps me from actively searching for another relationship. Concerned about my sexual needs, my daughter (a gynecologist) gave me a multi-attachment vibrator and laughingly said, "Have an orgasm Mom, but don't bother calling me in the morning." I followed her advice, but called to thank her anyway.

No Sweat Routine: Now that I have my trusty vibrator, I use it regularly. I'll take my fingers then tug, tap, stroke and so forth while resting the pulsating general massage tip on top of my hand. Amazingly, the feelings are heightened when I move around instead of just lying there. Unfortunately, I didn't always derive this much pleasure during sex with my late husband, whereas, time spent with my vibrator is always satisfying. It's just what the doctor ordered!

Name: Rochelle   **Age:** 31

Marital Status: Married

Children: 2   **Profession:** Accountant

Profile: My husband frequently travels on business and often meets available women. Although we have a great marriage, realizing men will be men, I make sure our sex life's exciting. He jokes that I always have a new trick up my panties and eagerly returns home to see what it is!

No Sweat Routine: My growing toy collection is a buzzing assortment of spirited delights. I've bought every imaginable vibrator and vary their use. We dress up, improvise with props and make erotic videos. While grocery shopping, I look for ideas to whet the sexual appetite. For example, as an alternative to massage oils and scented lotions, we'll use the wide flat tip on my multi-attachment vibe and spread mocha frosting over erotic areas, then lick it off. Great fun . . . worth the mess and calories.

A Girl's Best Friend?

Are diamonds still a girl's best friend? Because there's a lack of available men (especially Sugar Daddies) along with the fear of STDs . . . I doubt it! Let's get real. A hard man may be good to find, but a vibe is lots easier to come by. That may be why joy toys, not boy toys, keep a sparkle in our bedroom eyes these days. Don't get me wrong—I know a massager **can't** replace the tenderness, touch and affection of a real man. On the other hand, a machine has many stimulating possibilities. Let's have fun deciding who's top banana.

Men are *bedder* than vibrators because they can:
- ❤ Hug, kiss and caress you.
- ❤ Sweep you off your feet, or at least sweep the floor (sometimes).
- ❤ Play Scrabble, Sorry and Strip Poker with you.
- ❤ Take you to dinner, dancing or Disney World.
- ❤ Listen to your problems then offer a shoulder to cry on.
- ❤ Can be blamed for not paying bills on time.
- ❤ Jump your car or your bones.

Okay, guys, before you get a big "head," read the flip side.

Women prefer vibrators because they:
- ❤ Won't ask, "Am I the first, biggest, best."
- ❤ Don't care if you throw fits, have zits or feel like the pits.
- ❤ Never need to call his wife, kids or the shrink.
- ❤ Will not let you down or the toilet seat up.
- ❤ Can't abandon you for another woman . . . or man.
- ❤ Haven't a reason to take your tweezers or last razor blade.
- ❤ Eliminate risk of infection and rejection.

SeXercise, Socialize and Fraternize

All kidding aside, if you have a Mr. Wonderful, your vibrator can add variety and verve to partnered playtimes. Presented in a light way, it's not difficult convincing your guy to befriend a surreal surrogate. In spite of many men's fear about being replaced by a machine, once properly introduced, they're delighted at the difference it makes in a relationship. For example, vibes 1) eliminate performance pressure, 2) almost always guarantee **you'll** reach orgasm and 3) feel fantastic on him, too. Let's peek into Renee and Ray's boudoir to read how they recharged a rather routine rapport.

Joyzzz 'R Us

"Ray and I have been married 18 years. The last five we've been in a sexual rut. Like programmed robots, we made love once a week. He'd squeeze my breast, I'd stroke his penis. He'd play with me down there, then we'd roll together. After a few minutes, the hoopla was over. Would you believe, our only variation was "who's on top?"

One day a gal in my office arrived all excited because a store was running a sale on rechargeable wands. Since the price was low, she planned on purchasing two. Not sure anyone even needed one massager, I commented that getting two was a waste of money. Defensively she retaliated, "Obviously, you've never used one sexually, have you?" The answer was written all over my face. She proceeded to tell me how she not only used it sexually on herself, but on her boyfriend too. She divulged a few how-to tips which convinced me to buy one. That night, while Ray was out playing bridge, I tested the vibe and I couldn't believe how good it felt. Within minutes, I had a huge orgasm . . . the first in a long time! A few weeks of practicing on my own gave me confidence to share my private pleasure with Ray.

Initially, I gave him a nonsexual massage which he thoroughly enjoyed. Later, I lured him in the bedroom to massage my back. As he moved the wand over my buttocks, I ask him to pause on my upper thigh. I moaned and invitingly spread my legs a bit more. He got the hint. I rolled over and placed his hand on my clitoris with the vibrator atop it. Tingling sensations flowed down through his fingers and on me. My wild reaction excited him. Instinctively removing his hand, he made direct vibrator contact and I exploded in ecstasy. After catching my breath, I took the massager and lightly stroked his erection. He was thrilled. We're ecstatic thankful that electronic erotica had generated new life into our relationship."

Here's how to get the best of both worlds using your numero uno vibe with your number one man.

How to Rub Him the Right Way

Invite your special man to an evening of sensual, **not** sexual massage. Let him know the goal is pleasure, not performance. It's **his** time to enjoy and he's not permitted to do anything, including touching you. Set a mood that's conducive to relaxation, privacy and intimacy. Dress comfortably, but coquettishly, in something you can move about in and shed fast (if you catch my drift). Don't forget scented powder or oil, the latter warmed in your hands before applying. That's it, except for the vibe you're going to massage him with. Now use your feminine wiles to coax your honey and get him *hummmming*.

1. Show your partner the massager. Let him feel vibrations against his arm then have him lie face down.

2. With vibe on lowest speed, begin massaging shoulders, neck, back and arms. Slide assertively, but gently along. Use long strides, feathery strokes and circular motions, varying speed and pressure as he relaxes.

3. Gloriously glide massager down, paying particular attention to buttocks, upper thighs, lower legs and feet.

4. Now roll him over for a **non-genital** frontal caress. Stroke vibrator over chest, nipples and undersides of arms. Play the seductress with finesse. Allow your hands to become extensions of your adventurous spirit while immersing yourself into the erotic energy.

5. Talk softly, mixing massage with kisses, tongue flicks and nibbles on neck, ears and belly. How's he doing?

6. Move along working vibe up and down inner thigh. Stray playfully around **not** on genital area. (Broad hint: it's okay to accidentally brush his penis with your free hand, but not with vibe.)

7. Watch for signs of his willingness to participate. For example, nipples become erect, skin gets goose bumpy or, best of all, "Mr. Happy" rises to the occasion.

8. Don't be discouraged if he hasn't responded—you'll woo him over eventually. Keep in mind that a physical encounter not ending in orgasm is the foundation for heightening anticipation and the promise of things to come.

After finishing with the massage, teasingly say:

"THAT'S ALL FOR NOW"

In other words, if you see he's more relaxed than turned on give him a hug and kiss then leave him lusting for more!

Or, if you're into vibes and he consistently refuses to participate, tell him:

"PUT AND EGG IN YOUR SHOE AND BEAT IT BUD"...

When clitoral stimulation is the only was you can climax, why continue a relationship with such an insensitive man?

Or, if he's got a big grin and looks willing, murmur:

"WOULD YOU LIKE MORE SEXY STIMULATION?"

If he replies "Yes," you've got him in the palm of your vibrating hand. Continue onto seduction with erection.

Massage for Penis Captivus

Here's how to entice lover boy to enjoy a highly erotic *ménage à toy.*

1. Gently lift testicles. Use one hand to cup them while the other hand slowly sweeps vibe back and forth along perineum. Don't get overzealous and put the massager directly on his "man-thing" yet.

2. Place your mouth on his penis and press vibe against your cheek. He'll feel the rhythmic pulsations.

3. By now he may be willing to let you do anything to his "pride 'n joy," including direct stimulation but, uh-ah, don't be tempted. Instead, soften vibrations by placing massager atop the hand strok-

ing his penis, or cushion it with soft fabric. Better yet, slip off your panties and playfully wrap them around his penis before stroking with vibe.

4. Within a short time, your pampered partner will become acclimated to gentle direct (and erect) contact and be willing to include your joy toy in future fun and frolicking.

Uni-Sexy Toy for Two

Now that he's ready, willing and daring to get revved up, watch out—the best is yet to come! All types of titillating vibes can be used to turn on a routine relationship and spice up a super one. Here are ways to shake, shimmy, move 'n groove together:

1. Play a game of show and tell, showing him how you use the vibrator on yourself. Next, it's his turn to demonstrate what stimulates him *here, there* and *everywhere* using the massager.

2. Duplicate what you learned from watching, and take turns "doing each other." Add kisses, caresses and suggestive chitchat.

3. For a medley of sensations, get a his 'n hers pair of vibes (for example, one multi-attachment, one rechargeable wand). Use them simultaneously on yourselves, experimenting with all the attachments. Vary pressure, position, props and playthings. On your next come around, switch vibes, tuning into the different sensations each device delivers.

4. Watch one another use the massager. Only this time . . .
   - Test endurance and see who can last longest.
   - Try climaxing together.
   - See who can be a two (or more) timer.

5. Here's a tricky one: Stimulate yourselves just to the point of reaching orgasm, then **stop**. Put vibe down and make love. This is a great way for females to learn how to climax during intercourse.

6. For variety, or a safe alternative to intercourse, add finger or dildo penetration to mechanical stimulation.

Welcome to Adult Beducation

Whoever said "position is everything in life" was right. You don't, however, have to be an Olympic gymnast to use a vibe during intercourse. Of course, creativity, partner cooperation, playfulness, plus stimulating suggestions will catapult you both into pulsating paradise. With the ease, effectiveness and enjoyment vibrators bring to sexual scenes, even physically challenged couples, or individuals with sexual dysfunctions, will benefit greatly from adding playthings to playtimes.

"Welcome students. Fitness pro, Ms. Vi Brator, and myself, Mr. Buzz Zing, fitness erector, are going to teach vibrator lovemaking positions in the Couples Vibra-Sighs Class."

"Places everybody. Face your partner, select a technique (or improvise). With vibe in hand, begin."

POSITIONS 1-OH-1

1. **Missionary Accomplished:** Man's on top, female's below. Snugly situate vibe for simultaneous stimulation.

2. **Woman on Top:** She hops aboard and sits facing her partner or with her back to him. during penetration hold vibe against genitals.

3. **Doggone Good:** Bow-wow style with either of you holding vibe on clitoris will wow you over.

4. **Side Jobs:** She's on her back; he's on his side. Drape both legs over his thighs. Move massager pleasingly to orchestrate orgasm.

5. **Sexy Scissors:** Face each other lying sideways at right angles, with your legs opened in between his. Tuck vibe between pubes and press against them while rhythmically writhing and . . . (use your imagination from here on).

Rap Up

"Well done! Class dismissed! You may leave now, but do homework and, remember, practice makes perfect. Give yourself a pat on the back for completing the *Sizzlin' Sex* Fitness Program. Besides the physical and emotional rewards you've received, we're proud to present you with our graduation certificate."

SIZZLIN' SEX VIBRA-SIGHS

Congratulations to: _____
(*Your Name Goes Here*)

You are hereby awarded this **Suma Cum Loudly Certificate** for *sex-cessfully come-pleating* our no sweat, no pain, all gain, world-class regime. For adding muscle to masturbation, consider yourself certified in:

- Shaping up a saggy, draggy, lackluster sex life.
- Lifting spirits, stretching sexual savvy.
- Getting motor-vated to pump pleasure.
- Strengthening, tightening and toning bod inside 'n out.
- Dumping inhibitions, building self-confidence.
- Practicing **safe**, satisfying sex with lean, not-so-mean machines.
- Achieving new levels of orgasmic heights through *auto-erotic* excellence.
- Cross-training by varying joys, toys and ploys.
- Going the extra mile while performing regular workouts.
- Mastering "wait" loss (a.k.a. instant gratification).
- Performing dynamic upper and lower body *seXercises*.
- Exercising options to share work-ups with a fellow classmate.
- Enjoying stiff competition . . . when the occasion arises.

Zeal of Approval

Vi Brator
_____
Ms. Vi Brator
Fitness Pro

Buzz Zing
_____
Mr. Buzz Zing
Fitness Erector

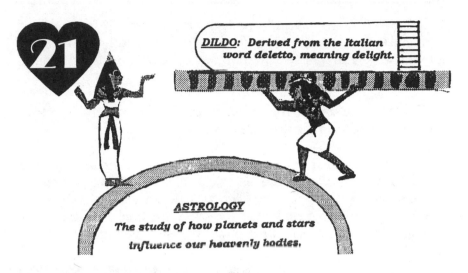

DILDO: *Derived from the Italian word deletto, meaning delight.*

ASTROLOGY
The study of how planets and stars influence our heavenly bodies.

Dildos—
The In Things

Historical and Hysterical In-puts

Think dildos are a recent innovation? No way! Phallic-shaped devices have been around delighting damsels for at least 2,500 years. In fact, they can be traced back as far as the birth of astrology. Hardly a correlation you say? Don't be so sure. It may be a question of which came first—star-gazing or satisfying sensuous stirrings with an ancient insertable. Check out the phallic facts, not fallacies, to see how they measure up:

☆ 1300-1236 BC (*Before Cucumbers?*)—Dildos made of clay were placed in Egyptian tombs. In this era, Rameses II of Egypt established four cardinal signs of the Zodiac: Aries, Libra, Cancer and Capricorn.

☆ 1162-1120 BC—The Chinese created object d'art dildos carved out of ivory. While Babylonians wrote about a moon goddess Ishtar whose name was later changed to Venus. Alas, we know this ruler of love and fertility had her charms, but not her arms. (So much for Venus envy.)

☆ 500 BC—A Greek vase adorned with astrological signs depicted a woman inserting a dildo into her mouth while another penetrated her vaginally. The oldest horoscope ever found was dated around this time as well.

☆ 500 AD—Insertables continued to evolve. During this era they were fashioned from sealing wax to absorb body heat.

☆ 1162 AD—The French introduced long, flexible rubber dildos called "*consolateurs.*" These historic phallics were often equipped with a reservoir that could be filled with liquid and ejected via an attached pump. This play and spray device has been updated; however, the mechanics of astrology remain unchanged.

When adult toys finally arrived in America, dildos became a sign of the times. A new era of sexuality opened up and the rest is *his-tory* . . . and her-story too. Could there be one of these playful pacifiers in your astrological sign?

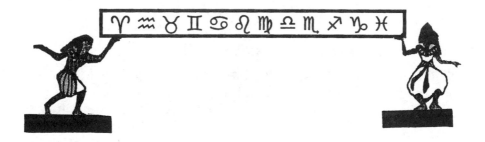

Destiny in Your Hands

If you dig dildos, you no longer have to dig deep in Egypt, take a slow boat to China, or ask your *mummy*. With the invention of synthetics, silicone and batteries, insertables are readily available and robustly realistic. These sexy superstars are available in a dizzying and delightful diversity of shapes, sizes, styles and colors. Widths vary from narrow, medium, wide and can't hardly fit through the door! Lengths measure in at micro-mini (2 inches) on up to Jumbo John (12+ inches) Holmes—even longer if it's double ended! Be prepared to pay by the inch; the bigger the size, the higher the cost. Ahhh, what price pleasure might be in your future.

ACCENTUATE THE POSITIVE

On the positive side, dildos are:

- Ready for insertion any time the urge emerges.
- Available in electric and battery-powered.
- Manufactured using a variety of materials from super hard to cushy soft.
- Inexpensive; can be purchased at your friendly drug store in the guise of a face massager (sure, sure).
- Offered in a humorous, humongous assortment to quench the fire of any desire.

The drawbacks are:

- Limited vibrations in some models make them inadequate for first-time orgasms.
- Many are noisy.
- Most suffer from shoddy workmanship, giving them a shorter life span than body massagers (a.k.a. vibrators)
- Batteries are unpredictable, tending to conk out as you're warming up (reminds me of some former dates).
- Sexy styles can only be found in adult shops or catalogs.

Sign of Venus ♂ Female symbol.

Sign of Mars ♀ Male symbol

Pre-dick-tions

Understandably, some people question the validity of astrology and need proof before believing. In our horoscopes, the planets merely indicate playful possibilities to enjoy one style of dildo over another. If you decide to spice up your sexuality with an insertable, our predictions help find the perfect toy for you. Purchase the dildo of your astrological sign then align *your* heavenly body with it. Although this unique match-making approach may raise eyebrows of astute astrologers, try before passing judgment. Even Janie, Joannie or . . . a Genie can't be totally accurate with general interpretations. But see how correct these descriptions are at portraying the way your sun sign affects your intimate pleasures: Besides, it's fun, and so are the following forecasts in this **dildo** prophesy-all and tell-all.

FIRE SIGNS

Leo
July 23-Aug 22

Aries
Mar 21-Apr 19

Sagittarius
Nov. 22-Dec 21

You have fiery enthusiasm for sex and are capable of receiving abundant joy.

AIR SIGNS

Aquarius
Jan 20-Feb 18

Gemini
May 21-June 21

Libra
Sept 23-Oct 23

You're romantic and adventurous.

WATER SIGNS

Pisces
Feb 19-Mar 20

Cancer
June 22-July 22

Scorpio
Oct 24-Nov 21

You're a sensational lover and often get what you want.

EARTH SIGNS

Capricorn
Dec 22-Jan 19

Taurus
Apr 20-May 20

Virgo
Aug 23-Sept 22

You love being admired and are curious about joys 'n toys.

Fact-Finding Mission

Is there anyone who hasn't snickered over silly ads for phallic-shaped "facial massagers"? Let's face it, the only way this device benefits facial muscles is by causing a smile when used as **in**-tended. This familiar plastic plaything has come a long way, and newer models offer much more to smile about. Here's the scoop on phallic stars:

Hard Plastic Facial Massagers

Even at highest speed, seasoned masturbators find they don't offer a large enough charge—especially if you've been spoiled by a skilled lover or body massager orgasms.

Check Out: Smooth or ribbed plastic in 5-, 7-, 8- or 10-inch versions. Battery operated.

Flexible Non-Vibrating

New-age materials are basically what separates these dildos from those found in Egyptian pyramids. Although many are molded to look and feel like the real Mr. Mc Coy, these dudes don't move unless you do. A nice feature is those made of silicone yield to body temperature as well as contours.

Check Out: Playful rubber dickeys which are available in widths and lengths of your dreams, including king-*sighs* double *dong-ers*.

Battery-Operated, Flexible, Vibrating Two-fers

These double delights shake, shimmy and rotate like the real thing. Popular models are shaped to keep the longer phallic form inserted while the smaller shaft hums 'n strums clitorally.

Check Out: Rabbit Pearl, Finger and Thumb, Man with Beaver and Pisces Pearl.

Electric Flexi Fun

Plug into cosmic, non-stop pumping. Unless there's a power outage, these dildos don't quit until you do.

Check Out: Up 'n Down, 8" Shaftman and 6" Clitterific.

Buzzing G-Spotters

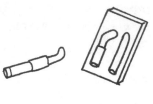

Optimally curved to reach in, touch, stimulate and turn on a world of G-spot fun. Makes finding that heavenly spot lots easier and delivers out-of-this-world orgasms.

Check Out: Flex-a-Pleaser, G-Spotter and Mini Vibe Kit with Flexy Finger Attachment.

Novel-Tease

More fun than swinging on a star, these "funzies" speak for themselves. What's in a name? See for yourself . . .

Kegelcisor. Unique and useful for toning PC muscle. This feminine fitness device is a weighty, chrome- and brass-plated dildo that functions as a mini vaginal barbell.

Anal Plugs. Vibrating and non-vibrating for a rare treat. The flared base keeps it from getting lost in "paradise."

Happy Tops. Pint-sized French Ticklers that slip over tips of plastic dildos. All are generously en-dowed with soft rubber nubs or bumps for a med-ley of sensations.

Sleeves. Latex sleeves dress up plain plastic dildos with bumps, grooves or curved tips to prickle your fancy.

Lighted and Glow in the Dark. Lost in the world of lust? Brighten sexuality and laugh all the way to orgasm with these glowing newcomers. Hard plastic, 7 inches long.

Of course, this is a mere microcosm of available models. Check out adult stores, catalogs and home parties for additional varieties. If you have a partner, it's fun to share.

Here's Darlene's experience after she read the following Virgo horoscope:

Horoscope

HAPPY BIRTHDAY
Virgo the Virgin!

VIRGO—Aug. 23 - Sept. 22
Your Birthday Today:
"This day's for dreams; the evening's for acting them out. Imagine something you desire and believe it will happen. Within a month, perhaps tonight, you'll meet a wonderful man whose first name starts with the letter "S." He'll be a smooth operator and very sexy. Since he's rather shy, it's up to you to be assertive."

ONE KNIGHT STAN

"Truthfully, I wasn't one to read a daily horoscope but it was my 39th birthday (again) so what the heck. My four-year relationship was kaput and I hadn't dated in ages. I remember wondering if I was destined to become my astrological sign, Virgo the *Virgin!* The only predictable event I had going was another (probably boring) gathering at a friend's home.

But it was there I met "him." At first glance he seemed so cold and detached it made me uncomfortable. A friend said I needed to loosen up. She was right, so I relaxed and tried keeping an open mind. He caused such a stir with the other women, it intrigued me. When no one was watching I moved in for a closer look and secretly touched him. His shape caused lustful sensations to course through my body. I had to have him. Nervous, but determined, we snuck out from the crowd; no one would ever know I was taking him home.

Hurriedly I drove away with my stud. Assuming he'd be history in the morning, I laughed as I dubbed him "One Knight Stan," figuring he'd be the proverbial *one night stand.* Arriving home, we made a mad dash to the bedroom. We were both ready.

Oh Stan, I sizzled at your touch. You sent passionate vibrations to every nerve in my body. I tingled with excitement when you aimed your hard throbbing shaft at my writhing pelvis. Continuous waves of pleasure engulfed me as I rhythmically moved against you. I moaned Stan, Stan, say you want me, tell me you care. But he remained silent, except for his slightly annoying, continuous "hum."

Becoming more assertive (as my horoscope suggested), I pressed Stan's firmness against my breasts. His good vibrations caused my nipples to swell. When I daringly inserted his pulsating erection, he responded by stimulating my clitoris. I couldn't hold back any longer and selfishly climaxed.

Afterwards, I jokingly tried to make light of the experience but he had no sense of humor. "Stan," I thought, "you're great in bed. Was it as good for you as it was for me?" Silence . . . Stan couldn't express himself. Even so, my body told me to keep the relationship going knowing there would never be compliments, phone calls or candlelight dinners. You see, not to put Stan down, but he can't do any of these things. If you haven't guessed yet, he's my "Knight in Shimmering Latex"—a darling **dildo**!

Chuckle all you want, but this type of relationship isn't silly. After all, he's faithful, into **safe** sex, accompanies me on trips and is willing and able any time my urge emerges. Furthermore, he couldn't care less about my age, weight, or the location of the remote control. No longer did I feel like "The Virgin." So much for astrology, I thought until . . .

As predicted, I actually met the real man mentioned in my horoscope, Stuart (with an "S"). Poor Stan, he's slightly neglected. I thought he was mad because he conked out during a hot session; I panicked assuming his little heart was broken. Fortunately, it was only a battery problem. I know I'll never give up my trusty toy completely; in fact, I've introduced him to my new guy and we're now a trio."

PS: As for astrology, I've become somewhat of a believer and regularly read my horoscope along with Dear Abbey.

Sign of the Times

Eager to know what the future holds? Hoping your stars can predict when you'll get the orgasms of your dreams? One thing's for sure: putting a dildo to the test will be an enchanting experience. Look over the info relating to your star sign. Perhaps the following phallic prophesies will enhance your earthly eroticism . . . believe it or not!

The Rabbit Pearl   **Aquarius**   **The Water Bearer** ♒
Jan. 20 - Feb. 18

Quietly independent yet a little eccentric, you thrive on the unexpected, disliking a set routine. As a free-spirited Aquarian, enjoy the flexibility of a seven-inch, silicone **Rabbit Pearl**. Plastic beads rotate against vaginal wall while little bunny ears simultaneously tickle clitoris. It's the "Bearer" of good vibrations, hare, there, everywhere.

Flex-a-Pleaser   **Pisces**   **The Fish** ♓
Feb. 19 - Mar. 20

Mmmm, what a hot number you can be. Have you ever had a lover who wasn't enthralled by the way you keep the action going? Since you're extremely intuitive and creative about satisfying your own needs as well, the **Flex-a-Pleaser** can send you into orbit. A small oblong sphere vibrates atop its long, slender handle curving into that hard to *G-et* at erogenous zone. It turns the "Fish" into a merry mermaid while she swims in a sea of sensuality.

Pisces Pearl   **Aries**   **The Ram** ♈
Mar. 21 - Apr. 19

You thrill at exploring new techniques, but lose patience learning them. Discover instant "sexta-sea" and catch a big one with **Pisces Pearl**. While the tail of an angel fish wiggles against clitoris, perky pearls vibrate within a 4 1/2 inch of silicone. Sporting a self-contained battery pack, it's the perfect catch for revving up a "Ram."

Up 'n Down Piston   **Taurus**   **The Bull** ♉
Apr. 20 - May 20

You're persistent about getting what you want, crave creature comforts and desire an affectionate lover with a slow hand. Because you detest being disappointed, rely on steady rhythms from an electric **Up 'n Down Piston** dildo. This one's pure pleasure, no "Bull" about it!

Mini Vibe Sexy   **Gemini**   **The Twins** ♊
Finger Attachment Kit   *May 21 - June 21*

What an impatient busybody you are! You find it essential to always stay in touch and know what's up. That's why the **Mini Vibe Sexy Finger Attachment Kit** will fill your bill of thrills. Let its fingertip reach in and stimulate you vaginally as the other end pulsates the clitoris. A magic touch for the "Twin" who enjoys doubling her fun.

Clitterific   **Cancer**   The Crab ♋
                                    June 22 - July 22

Ahh, Ms. Sensitive, so tuned in to the feelings of those around you. Your need to nurture is only surpassed by your aversion to boredom. Break away from stress and enjoy six inches of **Clitterific** satisfaction. It gives nonstop, AC action vaginally and clitorally, assuring you'll never be "Crabby" after a self-pleasure session.

 Finger with Thumb   **Leo**   The Lion ♌
                                             July 23 - Aug. 22

Loving, loyal, generous and oh-so spirited describes you perfectly. Knowing how trusting you are we offer a crowd-pleasing toy called **Finger with Thumb**. While the finger pulsates vaginally, the thumb fondles your clitoris. Easy to see the *main* event is shaping up for this "Lioness."

 Kegelcisor   **Virgo**   The Virgin ♍
                                        Aug. 23 - Sept. 22

With such an analytical, orderly nature, results are the name of your game. Organize and beautify your boudoir then jump in bed and tone up your sexual muscle with the **Kegelcisor**. Instantly feel its enhancing effect and the outcome will be amazing. It's apparent the blushing "Virgin" is shaping up to party hearty.

 G-Spotter   **Libra**   The Scales ♎
                                      Sept. 23- Oct. 23

Lovely Libra, your charm and gentleness attracts many admirers. You strive for fairness and compromise but secretly desire more independence. Turn yourself on with the softly curved, latex six-inch **G-Spotter**. Reach in and massage that specific G-spot until overflowing with joy. That's tipping the "Scales" in your favor.

 Squirmy Shaftman   **Scorpio**   The Scorpion ♏
                                                   Oct. 24- Nov. 21

Being the femme fatale of the Zodiac you get what you want and can't be easily fooled. Have we got a dildo for you! An electrifying eight inches of **Squirmy Shaftman** will satisfy devilish desires and make your "Scorpion" tail quiver delightfully.

 Man with Beaver   **Sagittarius**   The Archer ♐
                                               Nov. 22- Dec. 21

Aren't you the life of the party with your chatty, fun-loving nature! Hard to believe such a people pleaser values her freedom above all. Given your love of nature and animals, nothing's more perfect than the insertable four-inch hunter standing aside the squirming **Beaver**. It evokes simultaneous vibrations inside and out. Wow, the "Archer's" about to find her mark!

 Light-Up   **Capricorn**   The Goat ♑
                                      Dec. 22- Jan. 19

Here's a hard-working gal who pursues her goals with determination. Your high standards leads to a tendency to judge things by their usefulness. Indulge the need to lighten up by letting a seven-inch **Light-Up** dildo get your "Goat." *Ewe* shouldn't be sheepish—this one's ba-a-a-d to the bone(r).

Smart Moves

Enjoy future fun for two or one by pursuing these pertinent pointers:

* ★ Mutual masturbation is 100% **safe sex**. If, however, insertables are shared or used anally, slip a condom on dildo to minimize risk of disease.
* ★ To ease insertion and help eliminate dildo irritation, apply water-based lubes. Petroleum and oils damage latex.
* ★ Use alkaline batteries for optimum performance, but remove them if insertables aren't used regularly.
* ★ Dildos made of porous latex materials are difficult to clean and retain a less-than-fragrant aroma.
* ★ Here's a neat trick for keeping dildos, sleeves, etc. pristine clean. Unless AC or DC powered, sanitize on top rack of dishwasher. Pop small parts into nylon mesh bag or mini washer basket then wash separately from dishes.
* ★ For more info regarding cleaning adult toys, refer to the chapter on vibrators.

Guaranteed Good Luck

Ancient mystics and many of the present day populous still believe that what takes place in the sky touches their everyday luck, loves and lust. Universally accepted, however, is the theory that success in any endeavor is largely a matter of personal effort. You may seek an astrologer to predict how planetary movements will make your sexuality soar. With dildo in hand **you** have the power to make stars shine brighter and the earth move . . . if only for a brief moment in time.

Vaginal Balls—Have-a-Ball ... or Two

DOG-GONE,
She's Wearin'
Her Ben-Wa
Balls Again!

What Goes Around Comes Around

Think joy toys are something new? No way. For centuries vaginal balls were fashioned and fiddled with throughout Eastern Asia. Many a wise Oriental woman used them to relieve sexual tension while her husband journeyed off to erect a wall ... or something. Whenever an urge surged, the lusting lady could reach into her bag of goodies and come up with two cherry size metal balls. After inserting them vaginally she would wile away the hours blissfully. It's rumored that Ben-Wa balls were the reason Oriental women took small steps and smiled softly.

A Golden Oldie

Originally, vaginal balls were made of real gold. They were worth their weight back then but times have changed. Newer models are molded of plated metal or plastic and vary in diameter. They're normally sold in pairs and packaged in a fabric pouch or plastic case.

A New Ball Game

Thanks to Yankee ingenuity, new versions of this old pleasure have emerged. Now you can get on a sexual roll more easily and effectively using round, bullet or battery-powered egg-shaped devices. No doubt you'll find something enjoyable on the menu of Far East fare. If you have a yen, give them a try. And if I see you smiling while walking with small mincing steps, I'll understand.

BEN-WA CUISINE

Heat In ♥ Take Out ♥ Fast Delivery

Combination Specials* (Spi-ce-me)

#1 BEN-WA   *SUM - CUM - TOO*
Two small, gold-plated, heavy steel balls, for vaginal use only. A waitress told me they excited her sexually since they moved around as she worked. Laughing was difficult, because unless she remembered to squeeze her PC muscle, they'd come bouncing out . . . "S'cuse me waitress, there's a Ben-Wa in my soup."

#2 DUO TONE   *RUC - N - ROLL*
Two hollow plastic balls, about 1 1/2" in diameter, tied together by nylon cord with Ben-Wa's sealed inside. They give more bounce to the ounce. Travelers beware, steel balls can set off a metal detector, and airport scanners may uncover your secret. The handy cord lets you yank them out in a hurry . . . small consolation!

#3 THAILAND BEADS   *PAK - SUM - TWAT*
A series of mini plastic beads evenly spaced on nylon cord. Insert, then pull out slowly during orgasm. If you'd like a rare treat, buy another set for anal use.

Vibrating Specials ** (Waa-tu-go)

#4 ECSTASY EGG   *SUM - CHICK*
A single battery-powered plastic or metal-plated egg-shaped device. High-powered vibrations soothe your insides like a steaming bowl of won ton soup. Similar to all vibrating Ben-Wa's, the power cord hangs out and is attached to a variable speed control. Use caution when pulling the wire to remove, or you'll surely break the heart of this little buzzer.

#5 SILVER BULLET   *SO - LO - CUM*
Same delight as above only bullet-shaped.

#6 DUAL DANCERS   *GOO - IN - YU*
The house special. A pair of plastic or silver-plated bullet-shaped devices to double your good fortune. If you please, insert one vaginally, the other anally.

* Savor alone or with a partner.
** Very satisfying and you won't be hungry in an hour.

Dish Up Some Fun for One

Keep Ben-Wa or Duo Tones at home, in the office, or take "them" on the road. No one will suspect your secret pleasure as they quiver deep inside when moving or driving about.

Squeeez Pleeez

Exercise your right to a toned up bod, inside and out. Simply slip in the spheres then stair-step, dance or jog. Insert balls then flex-ercise your PC while using weights, biking or hiking. This adds a new slant to your exercise program.

BEN-WA BALLS INSERTED

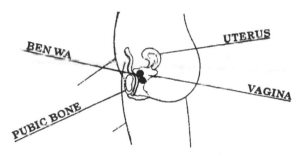

She's Only Rock 'n Roll

Get into the swing of things with a rocking chair or hammock. Insert balls, get comfy, then rock to and fro while reading or viewing erotica. Close your eyes and fantasize. Fasten your seat belts— it's gonna be a bumpy ride.

Home Sweet Home

Has housework got you down? Pop in a pair of balls while dusting, washing dishes or vacuuming and kiss drudgery good-bye. Maybe I'll start doing windows again . . . no way.

Hop to It

Vaginal balls are perfectly safe, even if one or both gets temporarily lodged inside. When this happened to me on the first go-round, I tensed up and hopped around like a Banshee in heat. The minute I relaxed, squatted down and pushed out on my PC muscle, the balls came tumbling down!

Pulling Your Own Strings

Lisa M., a Miami stockbroker, enjoys her far-out, Far-East toys better than chop suey. Her favorites are Thailand Beads and Duo Tone. After inserting one or the other, she rolls on her tummy and uses a 7-inch vibrating dildo to reach "orgasmic heaven." Next, she tugs on the cord which creates additional waves of pleasure. Lisa loves inserting the vibrating bullet during intercourse but cautioned it causes her partner to climax instantly.

Find out if Ben-Wa's are your cup of tea. C'mon cookie, spice up your one-play with Oriental fun and give new meaning to the phrase AAAH-SOOO!

Inflatable Dolls— Have I Got a "Guy" for You

Best Man for the Job?

Looking for love in all the right places and still no luck? Not to worry, have I got a "guy" for you. The hunk I'm referring to is a lifelike, less-than-life-size material man. Not your ordinary dummy, but a pseudo-sophisticated model. Before you say, "no-way," let's see how *rubber Romeos* can be sexy companions.

A Hard Man's Good to Find

In some playful ways, male love dolls have advantages over real live lovers:

1. They eliminate the fear of rejection or infection.

2. They won't turn out to be "hunks from hell."

3. They don't ask your age, sign, or "was it as good for you as it was for me?"

4. They're always ready, willing, and able with inviting smiles and full-blown erections.

5. They never fall asleep when it's over, leaving you on a wet spot lusting for more.

6. They don't rush things, then jump up and go home to their wives.

The down side to this pretend partnership is:

1. They can't hug, kiss or whisper sweet somethings in your ear.

2. They won't send flowers or call the next day.

3. They can be dressed up, but you can't take them out . . . just like some of my dates.

4. They may say, "Not tonight *doll-ing*, I've got a puncture."

This Good Man's Not Hard to Find

Inflatable dolls are found hanging (and I do mean *hanging*) around adult sex shops or can be ordered through specialty mail order catalogs. Basic models are fashioned in beige or black, durable, washable rubber. All have painted on hair and facial features. Their main claim to fame is a welcoming mouth, anal opening, and stay-put inflated penis (*minus* the inflated ego). Bare in mind, these *bucks* don't come cheap.

The old adage "you get what you pay for," really applies to these faux fellas. For a pittance extra, your doll-ing sprouts synthetic hair and a mustache. More pricey are deluxe dudes offering velvety skin (feeling more like the real thing). Sexually speaking, he's enticing with his battery-operated mouth and movin', groovin' tight end. He'll *full-fill* every fantasy with his spectacularly endowed 9-inch, realistic (ha-ha), vibrating penis.

Note: For those wanting to get together with the girls, blow-up babes abound. They sport three openings: luscious mouth, love tunnel and darling derrière. Also up for grabs are their highly inflatable bosoms. (Wish my boobs could inflate as easily as theirs.)

How to Have Your Way with These Dudes

Silly as it sounds, even with his plastic personality, it could be heaven having this man around the house. Here are some *sex-successful* ways to toy with your boudoir buddy:

1. Plan the evening as you would for a date: two goblets of wine, soft music, etc. Get into the spirit by dressing in sexy linge-

rie. For *'real'* appeal, dress him like an average Joe in a pair of black socks with skivvies dangling around an ankle. C'mon, get loose, and make it an outrageous experience. This is one time you can't lay back and let him do all the work.

2. You wouldn't have sex with a stranger, so start by giving your boy-toy a name. Think of someone you love, hate or fantasize about. Pet names I've been privy to are *Ram-Beau, Sticky Dickie, Captain Kirk, Bubba* and *Poopsie* . . . **Poopsie**? I call my **real man** and his **unreal** counterpart *Stud Muffin*—don't laugh, sometimes the three of us get it on together!

3. Slather lotion or oil on your bod or his, then rub shoulders and other good parts together. Insert his throbbing manhood into your love tunnel and wrap your thunder thighs around his tender loins. I promise, he won't say a word about cellulite . . . thank goodness!

4. Tying his arms together with elastic or bungie cord allows room for you to slip into his waiting embrace. In this position, his arms are hugging your boobs and your back is against his chest. Now, he can enter you from behind without danger of fallout. Moving rhythmically back and forth plays it right for orgasmic delight. Don't worry or hurry; take all the time you need. Unless you deflate his desire with a piercing scream, you've got all night.

5. Place a warm, wet sponge in your *"head"* honcho's mouth. Position him so you can comfortably lower your honey pot over his moist *"tongue."* Lickety-split, this one's a hit.

6. Has he been a naughty boy? You've caught him wearing your lingerie? Just maybe you need to whip the wimp. Use a feather duster or a foam paddle and show Bozo who's boss.

7. Put your plastic man in places where no dummy has gone before. For instance, hoist him in the hot tub, party naked in a pool, or bring that dirty dude in to your bathroom and shower him with affection— much more fun than a rubber ducky.

8. We've handled safe sex using a sterile surrogate, now let's talk safety when driving at night. Dress your playmate in a shirt and hat and buckle him in the front seat of a car. To anyone looking in, it appears your not alone. All kidding aside, this one's for real.

Not Tonight Doll-ing, I've Got a Puncture

FULL-BLOWN FUN

If he's treated you right
let him stay the night.

But if you've had your fill,
and there's no more thrill,
knock the wind out
of his sails and send
him on his way . . . WHOOOSH!

24

Pack Woman— Have Toys Will Travel

Don't Leave Home Without Them

More than ever before, women are traveling solo for business and pleasure. If you're often on the go and sexy toys are your bag, why not take along a dependable travel *companion* (of sorts)? Since suitcase space is limited, there's no need to schlep an entire fortress of fun stuff. Opt instead for only one or two favorites you'd miss most, then pack those along with clothes, camera and credit cards. Personally, I wouldn't leave home (for too long, anyway) without them.

A Mixed Bag

If the accouterments you take traveling require batteries, don't forget spares. To help keep playthings from petering out, choose alkaline batteries—they work better and last longer. When traveling abroad with plug-in toys, don't forget a converter. You may need one anyway for blow dryers, irons and such. Another

handy item is a 12-foot extension cord (a 6-footer may not get the job done unless it's a guy). It's almost impossible to move a hotel bed or night table to reach the outlet. They must bolt the furniture. (TVs and lamps I could understand, but beds?)

Pack It All In

If packing a breakable toy such as a vibrator, cushion it with bubble pack or bulky items of clothing. I previously used tennis socks (clean ones, honest), stashing all sorts of items inside before rolling them up. Since becoming a shoulder pad junkie, I now use the pads to protect my toys in transit. Transfer love oils and lotions to travel-sized plastic containers. Secure tops then pop them into watertight, zip-lock bags. Before getting your show on the road, stash all sexy stuff in a non-revealing case. This is a lot less embarrassing if luggage is inspected.

Just in Case

If you're a frequent traveler, keep a spare set of toys and joys pre-packed, ready to go overnight or overseas at a moment's notice. Place this mini collection in a small case secured with a lock. One with a combination eliminates lost keys and affords total privacy at home or away. If you're a *frequent sigher*, check our naughty but nice list before you get packing:

TOO GOOD TO BE FORGOTTEN

- ☐ **Electric Vibrator**
- ☐ **Mini Vibe**
- ☐ **Rechargeable Vibe (Charger)**
- ☐ **Dildo**
- ☐ **Extension Cord (12 feet)**
- ☐ **Converter**
- ☐ **Batteries (AA, C, D)**
- ☐ **Condoms**
- ☐ **Handy Wipes**
- ☐ **Sensual Lotion/Oil**
- ☐ **Rubber Gloves**
- ☐ **K-Y Jelly**
- ☐ **Erotica (Video, Books)**

A Gift That Gets You Going

I've found the consummate travel companion. Much like a pocket flashlight, it's a 4-inch mini vibe that's mega powerful. Trust me, this featherweight baby packs a wallop on a single AA battery. Perfect for massaging tired tootsies after trekking around Tangiers or relieving *all sorts* of *ah, um* tension after business in *Bangcock* (oops, Bangkok)!

WHAT'S BUZZIN', COUSIN?

7:18 AM: My globe-trotting cousin Mandy, a successful lawyer, is dressed for travel: tailored suit, sensible shoes, hair neatly pulled back in a bun. She's leaving on an extended business trip and, pressed for time, packs hurriedly before catching her 10:35 AM flight. Mandy momentarily hesitates debating whether or not to take along the mini vibe I'd recently given her. As an afterthought she tosses it in her attaché thinking, "What the heck. With my pending schedule, I'll need a tension reliever." She locks the case and goes on her way.

9:55 AM: Mandy arrives at the airport and plunks her attaché onto the conveyer at the security checkpoint. The jolting sets the vibe off causing inspectors to gather round and investigate the buzzing. Her attaché is seized, opened and the "dangerous" four-inch dildo removed. After being carefully scrutinized, it was returned to the red-faced lawyer. Mandy now removes batteries from absolutely everything packed.

10:20 AM: Case closed!

TRAVEL TIP

Remove batteries before packing toys to eliminate fear of setting off airport buzzers. Hopefully the only thing they'll set off is **you**. *Ciao!*

"Over Hill, Over Dale . . ."

Flying may be the fastest way to get out of town, but a majority of travelers, commuters and salespeople still use trains, cars and campers. Here's the best innovation yet for long distance traverlers and commuters. It's an ingenious, inflatable neck pillow that has a **removable mini massager** tucked inside a back pocket. Lightly fasten it around your neck to ease tension and relax nerves and muscles throughout your body. Deflate pillow to fit into purse or briefcase. Beware, this honey of a headrest is so relaxing you may miss your stop. All aboard!

One "Sighs" Fits All

Hint

Once in the privacy of your home or hotel, this mini vibe can be removed and rerouted to more intimate locations . . . catch my drift?

On the Road Again

Weary of driving long, dreary miles for business or pleasure? Traffic tie-ups got you down? Wouldn't you rather arrive peppy not pooped? If you've answered **yes** to these questions here's one possible solution—**auto-erotica**, AAAA rated and sure to perk you up. Read how Beth from Tampa deflates a high pressure routine:

MILES OF SMILES

My job as a sales rep has me traveling by car over 500 miles a week. Whenever I'm feeling tired and there's no safe place to stop, I reach for my rechargeable massager. The first areas I energize are the ｐessure points on either side of my nose. From there I move on to my head, neck, shoulders then alternate arms. As stimulation continues, I become fully alert again. Thinking safety first, I massage tension from my fingers by laying the vibrator in my lap and resting its oscillating head in my free hand. The pulsations increase circulation, totally revitalizing me. If the mood grabs me and the road ahead is clear, I'll cruise down to "Pubes Mountain" which gets me feeling mighty good all over, taking me the extra miles. The idea isn't specifically to get sexu-

ally satisfied (ha) but rather to continue being an alert driver (honest officer). At the end of a particularly long trip I was rewarded by a customer who commented on how perky I always arrive. "Just don't understand how ya do it," he drawls. "You otta pass 'round your secret cause lots of salespeople would be much obliged to learn." Would they ever!

PUBES MT

Stop, Look, Glisten and Feel Good

Before grabbing your keys and fueling up, let's review some *auto-erotic* rules of the road never taught in Driver's Ed.:

- ✔ Always think **safety first.** Lock doors, be alert, maintain posted speed and steer clear of drivers with prying eyes.
- ✔ Place *auto-erotic* accouterments in an easy accessible bag you can lock.
- ✔ **Beauty bonus:** besides keeping you perky and entertained on the road, massages help keep skin supple and youthful.
- ✔ Keep moist towelettes in the car. Facial massages are therapeutic only if pristine clean.

- Rechargeable vibrators are a primo way to go since there are no wires to cross you up. For uninterrupted pleasure trips, treat yourself to a convenient 12-volt adapter for recharging the vibe . . . and you!

- The mighty mini vibe can be inconspicuously tucked in an eyeglass case. If a personal *umm-urgency* arises, don't argue priorities—temporarily borrow the battery from your beeper. Get the message?

Life Savers for Land and Sea

When a hunk of opportunity honks, prepare for a quick getaway. If you're the outdoors type, keep a spare toy or two on your boat or camper ready for a spur-of-the-moment outing of sun, fun and then some.

THREE FOR THE ROAD

1 . . . if by land
2 . . . if by sea
Bring along a toy
    and make it
_____
3
Adds up to a fun trip!

A big 10-4, over and out!

25

Organize Your Toys— Social Security

Hide 'n Seek

If you have sexual accouterments (you do, don't you?), you'll need a convenient yet confidential storeage area. Ready and reachable for planned or spontaneous times—someplace out of sight, not out of mind. they'll add immeasurably to your solo or shared interludes. Why ruin the mood having to look for a toy you enjoy but hurriedly hid from curious children, a nosy roommate and the like? Until becoming organized, I was forever seeking places to conceal sexy stuff. Many times I wanted a plaything in a hurry and forgot where it was stashed. Has this ever happened to you? If so, end the frustration by arranging toys as you would clothes, kitchen utensils, office supplies, etc. Even if your collection consists of simply a toy or two, when the urge emerges it's nice knowing they're within reach ready for Freddy, Eddie, or **you** and you alone.

INSPIRATION FROM PERSPIRATION

Sharon is a forty something, feisty friend who lives with her cat "Smoochie." Because it's just the two of them, she lets her toys, clothing and cards fall where they may. At least that *was* true until the fateful furniture delivery day. When the doorbell rang, Sharon was on the phone. Letting the man in, she quickly motioned him into the direction of her bedroom. When he returned, minus the furniture, the young man had a grin on his face. "M'am," he said, "you single women sure are something." Sharon didn't think twice about his comment until he left and she went into the bedroom. There, in all its glory, was the evidence from the night before: an empty wine glass, the nude centerfold with his come-hither smile and . . . yup, you guessed it, a larger-than-life 10-inch terminator dildo. Sharon was humiliated, and since then has become much more organized. Thanks, Shari, for being the inspiration for this chapter.

Lock, Stock and Barrels of Fun Stuff

To keep toys tidy, borrow hints from Hidee:

- ♥ For those who regularly use an electric vibrator and privacy's no problem, keep it plugged in near the bed, but out of sight. Get in the habit of tucking the toy inside a pillow sham or under the mattress. You never know when unexpected company might drop in.
- ♥ If you can't keep the toy itself plugged in, keep an extralong extension cord in the outlet for a quick love connection.
- ♥ Vibrators, dildos and other playful paraphernalia can be stored in a covered basket, decorative box or, if your collection's humongous, a steamer trunk . . . just kidding!
- ♥ Keep battery-operated love-stuff clean and ever ready with extra batteries handy.
- ♥ Transfer sensual oils and lotions to unbreakable, flip-top or pump containers which can be kept on your night stand.

- Place small items such as beads, feathers, fluff 'n stuff in multi-pocketed, clear plastic organizers. They can be seen at a glance and they won't get lost in the shuffle.

- Are you a toy pack rat? Toss playthings that are broken, unsafe or no longer enjoyable.

- For neat, discrete storage of teasers 'n pleasers, transfer the kit 'n caboodle to an attractive lockable zippered bag. One with separate compartments is great for home or travel.

- Keep your erotic library current and clutter free. Instead of hoarding stacks of magazines and wasting time looking for the good parts, clip only the steamiest sections and favorite photos of centerfold hunks then place them in a folder. If you must save an entire book, mark hot spots with removable stick-on tabs.

- A night table with drawers makes a convenient toy catch-all, although the contents aren't immune from prying eyes unless it locks. My former neighbor cleverly solved her need for intimate storage.

Smile File

Nancy keeps a studio apartment in Manhattan which also doubles as an office. She solved her need for intimate storage by decorating a file cabinet then placing it alongside her sofa-bed. Both drawers lock; one holds standard business papers, the other hides her playthings. From 9 to 5 it all looks very professional, but after hours it's another story. That's because all work and no play makes Nancy antsy!

How I Skirted the Issue

My private collection was a jumble of toys, tangled cords and excess erotica. I got my accouterment act together by placing an inexpensive round table next to my bed. I covered it (and my tracks, too) with a floor-length skirted cloth. Underneath are three shelves: one for toys, another for lotions and notions, the third holds magazines and erotica. When settling down to sexy fun, I lift my "skirt" in more ways than one!

Table of Contents

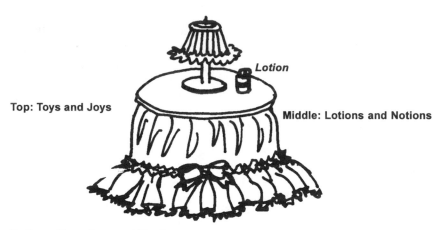

Top: Toys and Joys

Lotion

Middle: Lotions and Notions

Bottom: Magazines and Erotica

26

Hear Ye, Hear Ye

The Princess of Self-Pleasure Wants to Share Her Sizzlin' Treasure Trove with a Princely Partner.

Sharing Outrageous Orgasms—M'Lady Treats M'Lord

A Midsummer's Night Dream . . . Not Scream

Okay, you've been captivated by the sensational feelings sex-for-one elicits and it's your "secret" pleasure. Now you want to make merry and introduce a charming sire to mutual masturbation along with the *magical toy chest*. Alas, milady appears confused about what to say or do. Are you afraid your lord will become skittish and hurriedly gallop off in the moonlight leaving you horsing around alone? "Tsk, tsk, not to worry" we gallantly state. Before subjecting yourself to possible disappointment and becoming the town crier, we "beseech ye" to read further.

To share private playfulness (with the sire of your heart's desire), it "pleaseth" us to present declarations fit for a queen. You've awakened the scintillating Sleeping Beauty within and are now ". . . the sexy stuff dreams are made of." Why waste a precious moment in deception or despair? Let him meet the self-sensuous "other" woman (you) and . . .

Declare the Desire to Share

In order to form a more perfect union, insure domestic tranquility and promote sexual excitement, I _____ (*your name*), **Princess of Self- Pleasure**, by the powers of my new sizzlin' sensuality, do ordain and establish this allegiance for the *bedderment* of my intimate relationship(s).

Declaration for Sexual Independence

Fun-Official
Jack, Jill and Bill of Rights
A.K.A.
How to Introduce a Lover to Toys, Ploys and a Handful of Joys

Article I: Communicate with Your Mate

Understandably, most people are embarrassed to admit they masturbate, but, if you're wanting to spice up a shared sex life or are tired of faking it, you're gonna have to tell him. Whether a new date or long-time mate, some men may balk at the suggestion of partaking in self-pleasure *au deux* and using playthings. Use a come-hither strategy to entice and seduce him with the idea of trying something new and outrageous. Choose a relaxed setting and arrange to talk privately. Add provocative eye contact, compelling body language and dulcet tones to convey the excitement you expect to share.

Article II: Tell Him and Sell Him on the Idea

If he questions your motives, hug him dearly and emphasize that no man, especially him, can ever be replaced by a toy or ploy—absolutely, positively, that's not the intent. These devices are used **along with**, *not* **in place of** lovemaking to enhance and expand erotic enjoyment. Explain that couples who want to play and stay together pump up intimacy with a variety of adult games and accouterments. It's a refreshing leap from the dark ages of bedroom boredom and a **safe** way to initiate intimacy with a new beau.

𝔄rticle 𝔍𝔍𝔍: 𝔅enefits and 𝔖well-fare

It's understandable either of you may have reservations about shared masturbation and think it is a **no-no**?

But guilt, schmilt! In *mid-evil* times that sort of archaic thinking was acceptable; today, happily, it's gone out with the horse and buggy. Mutual toying and ploying can almost guarantee sexual satisfaction.

Be honest while talking about your sexuality. Explain how you've discovered what stimulates your hot spots and say you'd love showing him. Most men would rather have their partner masturbate than not climax at all.

Here are more reasons to unlock inhibitions, open up and share your chest of dreams and uni-sexy schemes:

❤ Does the trick when either is unable, unwilling, or too pooped to pop.

❤ Loverboy gets "permission to share his secret indulgence . . . (masturbation).

❤ Exciting way to eliminate risk of infection, pregnancy or physical discomfort.

❤ Both partners get a "bang" darn near every time.

❤ Bestows additional pleasures and mutually increases the intensity of enjoyment.

❤ If being together is impossible (due to business or other circumstances), bridge the distance by including self-pleasure with a lovey-dovey phone call. Just hope Ma Belle's lines don't fizzle while you sizzle.

Article IV: Show 'n Tell

Whether you have a castle in Spain, a condo in California or a flat in Flatbush, quit beating around the bush and get real! Tis true, the first time you masturbate with a partner might be embarrassing, but we're willing to wager a king's ransom that you can pull it off if ye wilst follow these royal guidelines:

Whether Lord, Lady . . . or Layperson, add richness to your roustabouts by sharing sexual solitaire. If at first ye don't succeed, try, tryst again!

Note: In our quest to keep this information hysterical, not necessarily historical, we apologize for murdering the King's English . . . did you expect Shakespeare?

PALACE PROCLAMATION

Thou shalt . . .

- ♥ Not ask him *if* he masturbates. (95% of males admit they do . . . the other 5% lie!)
- ♥ Beseech him to demonstrate how he fondles the family jewels (we know he does) then promise to return the favor.
- ♥ Titillate each other by reading erotica or watching X-rated instructional videos. Especially evocative are scenarios depicting mutual masturbation and sharing love stuff.
- ♥ Stock madam's chambers with a bewitching bevy of interacting accouterments: a lolla-palooza for him and a favorite for thyself.

Let's scale the palace walls and eavesdrop on how some of history's famous women handled their sizzlin' sex. These jolly good examples may inspire introducing your capers to an amorous courtier.

Long ago, regal ladies spoketh of orgies for one . . . and then some.

Elizabeth I (the virgin queen): "Men schmen, who needs 'em. Daddy's (Henry VIII) memoirs were reasons enough why I ner' wed. Besides, I learned to satisfy my passionate yearnings and oftimes had shown the eager courtiers how to trifle with my crown jewels."

Marie Antoinette: "With me egging him on, lover boy Louie showed me where and how enjoyed being touched. Because we were busy getting our jollies off neither realized the populace was starving. I should have decreed making whoopee was more satisfying than eating cake."

Wallis Simpson: "Prince Eddy fell so madly in love with my openness to self-gratification he became un-ruly. It was our uninhibited frolicking, however, that would have really made history!"

Ann Bolyn: "I should have known better than making a big deal out of Henry's difficulty having an erection. Things would have worked out if only we'd concentrated on self-pleasuring until he was ready. Guess I lost my head."

Queen Isabella: "I asked Ferdie to watch me do my own thing (if you catch my drift) and divulge if it turned him on. As a reward, he showered me with abundant riches and three ships for my good friend Chris to sail."

Queen Victoria: "Darling Albert was so thrilled with our lascivious lovemaking we pompously pleasured ourselves in every position. Masturbating reigned supreme and was how I reached orgasms fit for a queen."

HARK!!! I hear the vibrator roar!

Whether Lord, Lady . . . or Layperson, add richness to your roustabouts by sharing sexual solitaire. If at first ye don't succeed . . . try, tryst again!

Note: In our quest to keep this information hysterical, not necessarily historical, we apologize for murdering the King's English . . . did you expect Shakespeare?

Article V: Right to Bear Arms (a.k.a. Joy Toys)

When it comes to lovemaking, are you two ships passing in the night? (Pssst, remember the adage, "Use it or lose it"?) Encourage shared and solo sex as a quick fix. (Leave a note under his pillow attached to the vibe requesting he keeps it warm.) Give the green light to private pleasuring if you can't be together. The more titillation you give yourself, the more you'll want.

Article VI: Privileged Time

Use a calendar and mutually set a monthly date to celebrate your "duet *d' amour*" with a new toy or ploy. If time together is tight, this helps you keep on top of things while having a ball to boot. Take turns dreaming up dandy rendezvous that needn't be pricy to be spicy.

Article VII: Assure a Lifetime of Orgasms

Everybody is guaranteed the unalienable right to pursue sexual satisfaction solo or shared. Vibrators make this possible in good times and bad, through sickness and health, 'til *death* of the toy do you part (batteries or toys conk out . . . in which case replenish stock).

Article VIII: Boredom Prohibited

Amazingly, once you move from mundane to marvelous masturbation and begin looking for sexy diversions, they appear everywhere. (This is how strawberries and whipped cream became a delicious turn-on.) Many ideas can be full of surprises, slightly startling or downright silly. Not everything works all the time and you might end up doing nothing more than giggling wildly. Great! Laughter is the best medicine and a sure cure for the blahs . . . which may be terminal! If the fun gets kinky (a bit *dungeonous* perhaps), the rule should be: anything goes if thee and he agree.

Article IX: Comply, Don't Deny

Accept the fact that we don't live in a perfect world. Although condoms are effective 90% of the time, currently the best defense against AIDS and other STDs is abstinence, a monogamous relationship with an uninfected person, or (our personal favorite) mutual masturbation. Safely keep the festivities fanciful with playthings 'n ploys. Raunchy romping may not cure a washed-up relationship, but it can revive a soggy one. If your partner doesn't agree to sharing sexual solitaire, decide if you desire a lifetime of satisfaction or are willing to settle for a dead-end destiny with an inflexible fellow who couldn't possibly have your best interests at heart.

Article X: Nothing's Wrong with These Rights

Although somewhat revolutionary, these sizzlin' seductions—for one and then some—are totally safe, sexually satisfying, aerobic, politically correct, bi-lingual, express freedom of choice, enhance individuality, restore virility and vitality, give pleasure, take little or no effort, etc., so what's wrong with them? Not a darn thing. Who says you can't have it all? We and other women do, why not you?

Whether a singular sensation or part of a dynamic duo, with you writing the script, your story's sure to have a happy ending. *Joust go for it!*

Picture Yourself

NEVER-ENDING CLIMAX

In days of yore damsels indeed found sex a bore. No self-respecting lady dared mention the "M" word, or, perish the

thought, "touch down there." She feigned passion while Sir Lancelot, *Came-a-lot*. Thankfully, the age of faking orgasm is past. Good riddance to night after frustrating (k)night of suffering silently or being *throne* for a loop by lousy lovers. Celebrate a joyous renaissance by joining other modern maidens who revel in their right to luxuriate in lusty self-satisfaction. Then, if you choose, use our naughty but nice sizzlin' advice to capture and enchant the man of your dreams.

XXXXX'S 'n OOOORGASMS
Cricket & Ginny

P.S: Before putting this book to bed, as promised in the introduction, we guarantee* your satisfaction.

*It is hereby bestowed upon Princess _____ *(your name) by the powers vested in her sexuality, a lifetime of fulfilled desire with or without a sire. If not come-pletely satisfied, we'll refund your orgasm!*

We toad you, the days of kissing frogs in hope of finding a fairy-tale ending are gone.

Naughty Notations

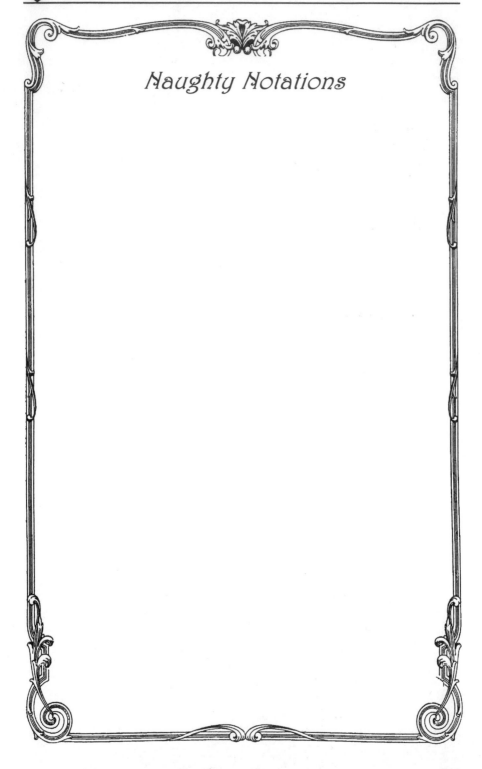

Naughty Notations